AIR CAMPAIGN

OPERATION
BLACK BUCK 1982

The Vulcans' extraordinary Falklands War raids

ANDREW D. BIRD | ILLUSTRATED BY ADAM TOOBY

OSPREY PUBLISHING
Bloomsbury Publishing Plc
Kemp House, Chawley Park, Cumnor Hill, Oxford OX2 9PH, UK
29 Earlsfort Terrace, Dublin 2, Ireland
1385 Broadway, 5th Floor, New York, NY 10018, USA
E-mail: info@ospreypublishing.com
www.ospreypublishing.com

OSPREY is a trademark of Osprey Publishing Ltd

First published in Great Britain in 2023

A catalogue record for this book is available from the British Library.

ISBN: PB 9781472856661; eBook 9781472856692;
ePDF 9781472856678; XML 9781472856685

23 24 25 26 27 10 9 8 7 6 5 4 3 2 1

Maps by www.bounford.com
Diagrams by Adam Tooby
3D BEVs by Paul Kime
Index by Zoe Ross
Typeset by PDQ Digital Media Solutions, Bungay, UK
Printed and bound in India by Replika Press Private Ltd.

Osprey Publishing supports the Woodland Trust, the UK's leading woodland conservation
charity.

To find out more about our authors and books visit www.ospreypublishing.com. Here
you will find extracts, author interviews, details of forthcoming events and the option to
sign up for our newsletter.

Title page photo caption: p.19

Acknowledgements
I wish to acknowledge those who helped make this book possible:
my son, Nick Bird, Tom Milner, Molly Chell, Bob Tuxford AFC, Dr Robert Lyman,
Rowland White, Adam Tooby, John Shields, Tim Ash, Pieter Johnson, Brian Armstrong,
Andy Barrett, Ash Holmes, 'Taff' Bland, John Hendy, Tony Ingelbrecht, Anthony Wright,
Andrew Dennis, Peter Devitt, Stuart Hadaway, Lee Barton, Guy Lemetayer, Paul
Alexander, Mark Willis, Carlos Mazzochi, Embassy of Brazil, London Luciana Paquet,
and Air Attaché Group Captain Cyro André Cru, .A. Moraes, Cel Av R1, Estado-Maior
de Aeronáutica, Brasil, Argentinian Embassy, London.

Author's note:
As the names of the islands are disputed, we refer to 'the Falklands' from the British and
islanders' perspective and to 'the *Malvinas*' from the Argentinian perspective. Everything
that follows is, to the best of my knowledge, a true and accurate account of the events.
I have drawn on a variety of sources to make this a balanced view.

Times:
All times in this book are local, except
Zulu time (e.g. 1830Z), the military
term for UTC or GMT.
NB The time difference between the
Falklands and the British Task Force was
around three hours.

Author's dedication:
To those who lost friends and family in
the fierce actions fought at sea, on land
and in the air during the 74-day conflict.
And to those who still suffer today.
A total of 649 Argentines died in service,
as did 255 British servicemen.

CONTENTS

INTRODUCTION

At the end of the world, a little bit of empire lingers on in the Falkland Islands, an archipelago in the South Atlantic over which Britain and Argentina have been at loggerheads for more than 300 years, with both claiming sovereignty. The root of the problem over these clumps of rocks can be traced to the celebrated *Inter caetera* issued by Pope Alexander VI, who guillotined the lands that European navigators were starting to discover into two territories, one Spanish, one Portuguese.

Lines drawn (and then revised) went straight from north to south through what is now modern Portuguese-speaking Brazil, leaving land to the west of the line to the Spaniards. This included most of the South American mainland, whose conquistador armies had not yet arrived in Mexico or Peru. The 1493 document showed that on the Spanish side of the line, still undiscovered 400 miles off the future Argentinian coast, lay the cluster of islands that the British would name after the naval entrepreneur Viscount Falkland, and on which the French explorer Louis Antoine de Bougainville would name the first settlement Les Îles Malouines after St Malo, in western France. Spaniards would much later adapt the French name to give the islands the name Las Malvinas.

It is not entirely clear whether Portuguese or Spanish sailors sighted this archipelago or any other South Atlantic islands such as South Georgia. The English navigator John Davis, aboard the *Desire*, made the first confirmed sighting of the islands in 1592. The first known landing was by English Captain John Strong in 1690 at Bold Cove, Port Howard on West Falkland. Strong seemed unimpressed, noting that there was an 'abundance of geese and ducks' but that 'as for wood, there is none'. He charted the sound between the two principal islands, which he named 'Falkland Channel' (today known as Falkland Sound) after the First Lord of the Admiralty, Viscount Falkland, and sailed away. Sealers, whalers and penguin hunters from different corners of the globe became frequent visitors.

Meanwhile, British legislators in Canada systematically cleansed provinces and territories of Acadian people during the Seven Years' War, deporting some to France. These displaced people boarded two frigates at St Malo in the autumn of 1763 under the command of French

An earth mover clearing soil for the new US Army Air Force base, Wideawake, on Ascension Island that will become a joint US Air Force and Royal Air Force base. (Photo by Ivan Dmitri/ Michael Ochs Archives/ Getty Images)

Admiral Louis-Antoine de Bougainville, and sailed across the South Atlantic to colonize the 'Îles Malouines'.

Anchoring in Berkeley Sound, they rowed ashore and christened the landing spot Port Louis after King Louis XV and established the first settlement on north-eastern East Falkland in February 1764. While Port Louis flourished, the British in January 1765 established a base off West Falkland at Port Egmont, Saunders Island, with neither party realizing that a settlement existed on the opposite island. Here the first systematic scientific and meteorological observations were recorded in the Falklands. Saunders Island continued to be used by British sealers and whalers until Jacinto de Antolaguirre, one of two Spaniards to govern the Falklands (Las Malvinas), in 1781 sent Salvador Medina Y Juan with troops to Port Egmont. Their orders were to 'destroy every object found in Egmont as part of your reconnaissance of that area'. No opposition was evident. All houses were burned to ensure they would not be re-used, and the name plaque was removed by Salvador and presented to authorities in Buenos Aires, from where it was recaptured by the British roughly 30 years later.

Northwood Headquarters in Northwest London. As Headquarters of the Commander-in-Chief Fleet, the site was the controlling Headquarters for Operation Corporate, the Falklands War, in 1982. (Andrew D. Bird Collection)

Almost every year from 1782 an ice breaker from Buenos Aires arrived at Egmont to prevent the British from re-establishing their rule. However, as Spain's empire crumbled under Napoleon's occupation and the march of liberal ideas – encouraged by Britain and the United States – Spanish domination in Latin America dissipated. Spring 1810 saw sovereignty over the Viceroyalty of the Río de la Plata transfer to the successor state, Argentina. In 1823 Argentina appointed a governor of the Malvinas, Louis Vernet from Hamburg, Germany, although his appointment was never officially gazetted – and so was not strictly legal.

The Falkland Islands became a Crown Colony in 1840. Governor Richard Moody, with the cooperation of HMS *Terror* and HMS *Erebus* captains Francis Crozier

and James Clark Ross, had them surveyed for a new capital for the islands. Port Jackson was chosen for the proposed new settlement and wharf. Colonial Secretary Edward Stanley in London concurred. The little town was officially renamed (Port) Stanley in 1845 with the capital administration centred at Government House.

A century passed, in which Argentina maintained its claim to the islands. By 1946, Britain's Foreign Secretary Ernest Bevin could no longer rebuff Argentine claims like his predecessors. At the United Nations (UN) General Assembly, on 6 December 1946, Bevin finally gave a response, proposing to take the dispute over the Falkland Island Dependencies – South Georgia, the South Sandwich Islands and the area known today as the British Antarctic Territory – to the International Court of Justice in The Hague for mediation. On three separate occasions over the following years Argentina declined this proposal.

Concern in the House of Commons grew during the years 1946–48, over Argentinian scientific detachments in British territory in the Antarctic, including a known Argentine weather base at Gamma Island. By 1953, the number of unauthorized foreign settlements on dependencies of the Falkland Islands stood at 11 at the point when the Argentine dictator, Juan Domingo Peron, tried to buy the Falkland Islands. This offer was conveyed to Britain by Alberto Teisaire, at the coronation of Queen Elizabeth. However, Peron was told that the sale would cause the overthrow of the Churchill government.

Buenos Aires, anxious to recover the islands, now took the dispute to the UN. The UN decolonization committee C-24 recognized the existence of a dispute and invited both countries to enter negotiations over the islands' future. British politicians on a factfinding mission were baffled by the emotion in Argentina, whose people considered the Malvinas as an integral part of their national soil. Life and communications on the Falklands had changed relatively little since the first settlement was created at Port Louis in 1784. The only means of reaching Port Stanley was still by ship, even if it was now a monthly steamer from Montevideo, Uruguay.

The airfield at Port Stanley

The passage from Uruguay remained the only viable connection to the South American mainland. The situation where the Falklands remained unconnected by air was unsustainable, and, during the 1970s, the question of implementing a commercial air route to Argentina came to the fore. A dual air and sea service was proposed, and David Scott, Assistant Under Secretary of State at the Foreign and Commonwealth Office, brokered a deal to strengthen the country's social and economic viability with essential access to public health, school facilities and scholarships in Argentina. But with no sustained support through a dedicated funding stream, after two months first the steamer RMS *Darwin*, and then the amphibian Grumman HU-16 Albatross seaplane operated by *Líneas Aéreas del Estado* (LADE), the Argentine Air Force airline, ceased operating.

June 1971 in Buenos Aires saw the British Government and the Argentine Republic sign Communications Agreement Resolution No. 2065 (XX) whereby external communications would be provided to the Falkland Islands by Argentina. On 3 May 1972, Grup 1 Construcciones boarded an *Armada de la República Argentina* (ARA, Argentine Navy) naval transport coal ship, with their machinery, docking in Port Stanley on 9 May. The construction team built a runway and an airport road over a period of seven months using locally sourced materials. On 15 November 1972, the runway was inaugurated when the first Fokker F-27 arrived with 44 passengers on board. It was a day when many saw the Argentine and British flags flying together on the Falkland Islands for the first time. Twice-weekly flights at Stanley airport allowed islanders to travel directly to mainland Argentina for pleasure, schooling or university, or to grow their businesses.

An early link to the Argentine mainland in the 1970s from the Falkland Islands, a Grumman HU-16 Albatross seaplane operated by Líneas Aéreas del Estado (LADE), the airline of the Argentine Air Force. (Andrew D. Bird Collection)

In 1976 the airport runway was extended by Grup 1 Construcciones. Flights were improved in 1978 when Johnson's Construction was awarded the British government build contract for Stanley airport, with a spur road and a fuel storage capacity enlarged to 50,000 litres (11,000 gallons). When completed, the permanent runway was 4,000ft long and 150ft wide and could accommodate Fokker F-28 jets; indeed days before the official opening by explorer Sir Vivian Fuchs, the Argentinians successfully landed a LADE Fokker F28 Fellowship twin-engine jet on the new runway. This service, operated by the Argentine Air Force LADE, was the only air connection to the islands; it was maintained until spring 1982. The airport also accommodated the Falkland Islands Government Air Service (FIGAS) with its Britten-Norman Islanders and de Havilland Canada Beavers. Prior to hostilities the Royal Air Force began to use the airport, to supply and reinforce the British military garrison when necessary.

First conflicts

With the signing of the air communications agreement, David Scott grasped the olive branch from the Argentinians, with diplomats on both sides hoping to normalize the relationship. However, by 1975 tensions had resurfaced. Under the command of Captain Philip Warne, the British Antarctic Survey ship RRS *Shackleton* had been sent to conduct an economic survey of the islands, with the expedition as a whole led by Baron Edward Shackleton, the son of the explorer Sir Ernest Shackleton. The Argentine government reacted by promptly sending their destroyer ARA *Almirante Storni*, which on 4 February 1976 intercepted the *Shackleton* at sea 87 miles from Port Stanley.

Warne rejected the idea of being escorted to Ushuaia in Tierra del Fuego, and stayed on course for Stanley, whereupon salvos of 5in shells were fired across the *Shackleton*'s bow. Despite Warne signalling 'explosives on board', the Argentines fired twice more. Undeterred, Warne refused to submit, and the *Almirante Storni* continued to shadow the ship until it reached 'the Narrows', a strait leading to Stanley harbour. His cool-headedness earned him an OBE.

A month before this incident, the expedition leader, Lord Shackleton, had arrived with a team of economists to begin the factfinding mission. Forbidden to transit Argentina, the team flew to Brazil and joined HMS *Endurance* to reach the islands in January 1976. Prime Minister Harold Wilson was unaware that Shackleton's visit coincided with the 143rd anniversary of Captain Richard Onslow's repossession of the Falklands in 1833, and Argentina withdrew their ambassador in protest. Shackleton's report of 454 pages embarrassed the Foreign Office and Prime Minister Jim Callaghan's government, which had expected it to conclude that the Falklands had no future except by collaborating with Argentina. Instead, Shackleton called for the investment of £14m over five years, including, most importantly, £2m to extend the runway at Stanley airfield. Callaghan appointed Ted Rowlands, a junior minister, to be responsible for these 'bloody dots' on the map. Ted Rowlands was sceptical of some of Shackleton's recommendations, but won the islanders' trust by commissioning the building of the new runway and spur road at Stanley airport.

Negotiations for a solution saw Callaghan's resolve tested. Argentina sent scientists and military personnel to Southern Thule, one of the Falkland Islands Dependencies. The establishment of a base flying the Argentinian flag, *Corbeta Uruguay*, provoked a response from Britain. Captain Hugh Balfour led a British expedition to the Falkland Islands aboard Leander-class frigate HMS *Phoebe*, together with frigate HMS *Alacrity*, nuclear-powered submarine HMS *Dreadnought* and auxiliary ships, and set up a 50-mile exclusion zone. In New York Rowlands met Argentina's Deputy Foreign Minister, Captain Gualter Allara, at the UN in an effort to reduce tension and discuss fresh sovereignty arrangements in favour of Argentina. With mounting chaos in Britain and fear of losing the leadership of the Labour Party, together with geographic and anti-colonial sentiment at the UN, Callaghan, in a non-interference pact, let *Corbeta Uruguay* stay. It would be a prominent jumping-off point for Argentine Special Forces to land on South Georgia in March 1982.

The road to war

The fall of the Labour government in May 1979 saw Rowlands depart. The election slogan 'Labour Isn't Working' was not lost on the islanders 8,000 miles away. Their whole economy was on a knife edge, with income from the islands' principal product, wool from its 600,000 sheep, having plummeted by 20 per cent. Islanders were leaving, as the only future they could see was Argentina taking over. For children, teenagers and those in their twenties and thirties there was little to stay for.

The new British Prime Minister, Margaret Thatcher, appointed Rex Hunt, a veteran diplomat who had been Consul-General in Saigon, to the governorship of the Falklands. Hunt immediately hauled the Falkland Islands Company, which had held a Royal Charter since 1852, into the 20th century. He instructed its land agent to sell one of its farms to the Falkland Islands government in an effort to make the islanders more self-sufficient. Green Patch was split up into six farms of roughly 15,000 acres and 3,000 sheep apiece. For the first time, six families had a stake in their own land.

The Fisheries Conservation Zone, another recommendation of Shackleton's, also gained Hunt's backing, but the Foreign Office stonewalled the idea, not wanting to anger Buenos Aires. Argentina had expanded its Rio del Plata fishery using factory vessels stationed around the Falkland Islands. Argentinian offshore fleets, with or without factory vessels, caught 230,000 tonnes of fish in 1981 as opposed to 16,615 tonnes by the Falkland islanders. It was realised this sector, if licensed, would bring the island the equivalent of $28.2 million a year, but would cause serious tensions with the Argentine Junta.

Unknown to Rex Hunt, Foreign Secretary Nicolas Ridley had already spoken with his opposite number Carlos Cavandoli and agreed in principle to the transfer of sovereignty to Argentina, in an arrangement similar to the leasing from China of Hong Kong's New Territories.

In January 1981, discussions about sovereignty were curtailed in Stanley's Town Hall. Lacking Rowland's tact, Ridley's confrontational approach failed to convince the islanders, and he promptly left aboard an aircraft of LADE, to the sound of furious demonstrators and the rare sight of normally rather supine Islanders waving banners and fists.

Ridley was lambasted in the House of Commons about his 99-year leaseback scheme and responsibility was passed to Richard Luce, who began a series of challenging discussions at the UN in New York. The Argentines had expected for over 20 years that sovereignty would be negotiated and eventually granted. These talks in New York under the UN's decolonization auspices had been running intermittently since the 1960s, more recently through the mid- and late 1970s. There were signs beginning to show that the military dictator, General Leopoldo Galtieri, who had seized the presidency in December, was tiring of the standstill and turning towards a military solution in imitation of India's seizure of Goa in 1961.

Handley Page Victor XL162 was built in 1961, and served on No. 55 Squadron. It flew on *Black Buck 1*, then *2* and *6*, and finally on *Black Buck 7*. (Brian Armstrong)

Argentina makes a move

From the mid-1950s to the early 1970s, Argentina was a profoundly undemocratic country, ruled by a succession of military juntas that declared an all-out campaign known as the 'Dirty War' when as many as 30,000 Argentinians were 'disappeared', many of them kidnapped from their homes, brutally tortured, then thrown from aircraft into the muddy waters of the Río de la Plata. In December 1981, General Leopoldo Galtieri took over as president of the three-man junta, becoming the dictatorship's third military president. One of his first actions was to approve the setting up of a commission to prepare for the capture of the Islas Malvinas in June 1982, codenamed 'Plan Goa'. This plan was to develop into Operation *Rosario*.

An expedition to South Georgia by a scrap-metal merchant had made Galtieri decide on impulse to invade. As Argentina was a staunch ally of the United States and supplied military and intelligence aid to its covert war in Central America, Galtieri and most of his fellow officers were under the illusion that as Britain was losing interest in the area, the USA would acquiesce in Argentina's reclamation of the islands. At the time, Argentina's economy was suffering a huge financial crisis, with the economy in freefall and large-scale civil unrest. Operation *Rosario* presented the military regime with an opportunity to distract the Argentinian people and gain their support. Except that none of the senior Argentine military officers on Plan Goa had assessed that Britain would react to the invasion with military force.

By February 1982, Luce was in talks in New York with Argentina's Deputy Foreign Minister Enrique Ros. Both sides were resolved on finding a solution. This was rebuffed by Galtieri, a fax from whose government made it clear that the only end-point of any negotiations would be to recognize Argentine sovereignty over the Falklands. Weeks later, on Friday 19 March, Argentinians were landing on South Georgia. By 29 March intelligence had been presented to the British government indicating that the invasion of the Falklands was coming and would take place early on Friday 2 April. The previous weekend contingency plans by Argentina for the invasion had been made. Argentine forces landed west of Stanley, the largest settlement on the islands, after sporadic resistance in the small hours of 2 April and shortly after midday the population of 1,800 saw an Argentine flag raised above Government House. As the islanders awaited a response from Margaret Thatcher's government, Defence Secretary John Nott was one of those reaching for an atlas to clarify exactly where the Falkland Islands were.

CHRONOLOGY

1981

31 August — Vulcan Operational Conversion Unit disbands

22 December — Military dictator General Leopoldo Galtieri takes office

RAF No. 617 Squadron Vulcans disbands

1982

February — British diplomat Richard Luce at the UN in New York holds talks with Argentina's Deputy Foreign Minister Enrique Ros

RAF No. 35 Squadron Vulcans disbands

29 March — Intelligence reaches London that Argentina's military may invade Falkland Islands within 48 hours

31 March — RAF No. 27 Squadron Vulcans disbands

All training abruptly halted for Argentine Naval Fighter Unit 2da Escuadrilla Aeronaval de Caza y Ataque to prepare Exocets for operational use

1 April — Rex Hunt, governor of the Falkland Islands, warns of a possible Argentine invasion

2 April — Argentine invasion of Falklands

British Cabinet approves sending of a task force to South Atlantic

Hercules transports deliver vital supplies to Gibraltar for Royal Navy

3 April — United Nations passes Resolution 502 demanding Argentine withdrawal

5 April — Royal Naval Carrier group sails from Portsmouth

6 April — British government War Cabinet set up to provide day-to-day oversight of campaign

US President Ronald Reagan's administration divided over the conflict

7 April — US President Ronald Reagan approves peace mission by US Secretary of State Alexander Haig

9 April — Alexander Haig arrives in London and begins five hours of talks

Vulcan B.2s based at RAF Waddington chosen, modifications begin

10 April — European Community approves trade sanctions against Argentina

Argentine Super Étendard pilots begin air-to-air refuelling training with C-130K

11 April — Admiral Sandy Woodward requests plans for best use of Sea Harrier to attack targets in Falklands

Alexander Haig arrives in Buenos Aires

11 April — Argentine Exocet weapon system declared ready

12 April — Maritime Exclusion Zone (MEZ) radius 200nm (230 miles) around Falkland Islands

Argentine ARA *Veinticinco de Mayo* aircraft carrier seen as a threat if Super Étendard are able to launch

Alexander Haig arrives in London

14 April	Argentine Navy sails from Puerto Belgrano	28 April	Britain declares 200-mile Total Exclusion Zone
	Haig returns to Washington to brief Ronald Reagan	30 April	Alexander Haig's peace mission talks between London and Buenos Aires finally collapse
15 April	British destroyer group takes up holding position in mid-Atlantic	30 April–1 May	Black Buck 1 bombing mission against Stanley airport; Sea Harriers also conduct attacks; naval bombardments of the same area commence
	Haig flies to Buenos Aires		
17 April	Admiral Fieldhouse holds conference on Ascension Island with Admiral Woodward	3–4 May	Black Buck 2 bombing mission against Stanley airport
	Haig presents Argentine Junta with a five-point plan	13–14 May	Martel-armed Black Buck 3 cancelled. Rescheduled for 15–16 May, then cancelled due to decision to end the Martel option
18 April	Argentine aircraft carrier has engine trouble		
	1st wave of five Victor K2s deploy direct to Ascension Island	21 May	British landings on the shores of San Carlos Water
19 April	Argentines land on South Georgia	24–25 May	Black Buck mission planned and aborted
	Air Vice Marshal Michael Beetham outlines benefit of using Vulcan bombers against Stanley airfield	28–29 May	Black Buck 4 launched but aborted
		30–31 May	Black Buck 5 missile strike
	Argentine Junta response to Haig passed to London	3 June	Black Buck 6 raid strikes radar position in Stanley. Vulcan XM597 diverts to Brazil
	2nd wave of four Victor K2s deploy direct to Ascension Island		
		10 June	Vulcan XM597 flies back to Ascension
20 April	Plan for landing on the Falkland Islands (Operation Sutton) discussed	12 June	Black Buck 7 bombing mission against Stanley airport
	1st of three x MRR Missions flown in support of Operation Paraquet	13 June	Vulcan XM597 returns to Waddington
27 April	Cabinet in London gives approval for Operation Sutton	14 June	Argentine forces surrender
	Sir Henry Leach notes that it is vital to deny Port Stanley airfield to Argentines as soon as possible		

ATTACKER'S CAPABILITIES
Fighting an unexpected war

In 1982 Britain's Royal Air Force (RAF) and Fleet Air Arm were focused on their vital responsibilities within NATO; consequently, neither were prepared for an independent expeditionary war in the South Atlantic. Successive Defence Reviews since the end of the British Empire had brought reductions in budgets and capability, and there was a limited number of assets. The RAF had five long range aircraft types: the Victor, the Vulcan, the Nimrod and the C-130 plus VC10 transport available to conduct Operation *Corporate* (war in the Falklands). British defence policy had been focused on a potential European and North Atlantic theatre of combat; consequently, a solo British out-of-NATO military operation had not been envisaged.

The RAF's NATO responsibilities were to provide air defence over an extensive area of 500,000 square miles. By April 1982 the fixed-wing aircraft in service for this task and maritime duties comprised 12 aircraft squadrons on high levels of readiness; four squadrons of Nimrod long-range maritime patrol aircraft; two squadrons of Buccaneer anti-shipping strike aircraft, armed with Martel missiles and laser-guided bombs; two squadrons of Phantom FG.1s; two squadrons of Harrier GR3s for use in the close-air support role; four C-130 Hercules transport squadrons; and 14 VC-10 C.1 passenger aircraft; two Victor air-to-air refuelling squadrons; two Canberra PR.9 squadrons; and three low-level tactical Vulcan squadrons, in the process of being phased out and replaced by multi-role Tornados. The Royal Navy's Fleet Air Arm had three squadrons of Sea Harriers.

Of these types, only a handful were capable of flying missions in the remote and challenging conditions in the South Atlantic: the RAF's Hawker-Siddeley Nimrod maritime patrol aircraft; the Handley-Page Victor and Avro Vulcan, originally designed as nuclear bombers, with the Victor now serving as a tanker; the Fleet Air Arm's Sea Harrier carrier-based fighter; and the RAF's version, the Harrier GR.3. In addition, the Lockheed C-130 Hercules transport aircraft served in the South Atlantic. The C-130s ferried personnel and supplies from Britain to Ascension Island via Gibraltar and Dakar, and as the naval Task Force sailed south beyond Ascension, they were the only way to airdrop important supplies to the fleet.

Initially Nimrods and C-130s did not have the capability to undertake air-to-air refuelling, another legacy of operating within NATO. RAF aircraft operating over the South Atlantic out of Gibraltar relied on the assistance of two West African nations, Gambia and Senegal, for refuelling en route. During the conflict, air-to-air refuelling solutions were rapidly developed, as were extended-range fuel tanks for the C-130s.

Key to the whole operation was Ascension Island, 7° 56' south of the equator in the Atlantic Ocean. The island had been leased to the United States as part of the 'Destroyers for Bases' package in spring 1940.[1] The United States then built an air base on the island, known as 'Wideawake'. By the time of the Falklands War, the United States had been operating from Wideawake for 40 years, and over the years the runway had been extended, widened and improved to provide an emergency runway for Space Shuttle flights. The RAF and the naval Task Force would use Ascension Island as a staging post for storage and missions.

Contributions by RAF on Wideawake airfield, Ascension Island to Operation *Corporate*			
Squadron	Aircraft Type	Number	Operational Use
No. 1 Squadron	Harrier GR.3	2	Wideawake airfield air defence
No. 10 Squadron	VC-10 C.1	14	Brize Norton to Ascension air bridge
No. 47 Squadron	C-130 Hercules	3	Lyneham to Ascension Island air bridge / special ops
No. 70 Squadron	C-130 Hercules	3	Lyneham to Ascension Island air bridge / special ops
No. 55 Squadron	Victor K.2	10	Air refuelling RAF and Naval aircraft
No. 57 Squadron	Victor K.2	10	Air refuelling RAF and Naval aircraft
No. 42 Squadron	Nimrod MR.1	3	Maritime surveillance, co-ordination of air-refuelling communication hub
No. 51 Squadron	Nimrod MR.1	3	Maritime surveillance, co-ordination of air-refuelling communication hub
No. 206 Squadron	Nimrod MR.1	4	Maritime surveillance, co-ordination of air-refuelling communication hub

Avro Vulcans used in *Black Buck* raids			
Squadron	Aircraft type	Number	Serial no.
No. 44 Squadron	Vulcan B.2	2	XM597; XM612
No. 50 Squadron	Vulcan B.2	1	XM598
No. 101 Squadron	Vulcan B.2	1	XM607

Air defence and close air support from HMS *Hermes* and HMS *Invincible*			
Squadron	Aircraft type	Number	Aircraft carrier
No. 800 Naval Air Service	Sea Harrier FRS.1	12	HMS *Hermes*
No. 801 Naval Air Service	Sea Harrier FRS.1	8	HMS *Invincible*
No. 809 Naval Air Service	Sea Harrier FRS.1	8	HMS *Hermes* / *Invincible*
No. 1 (F) Squadron RAF	Harrier GR.3	10	HMS *Hermes*

The British command structure leading up to Operation *Corporate* saw Chief of the Air Staff, Air Vice Marshal Michael Beetham, acting as Chief of the Defence Staff on Wednesday,

---

1   In this agreement, 50 obsolete destroyers were transferred from the US Navy to the Royal Navy, in exchange for leases on British territory, primarily in the Caribbean, and basing rights in Newfoundland and Bermuda.

Victor K.2s of No 57 Squadron with serial numbers K.2 XL512 and Victor K.2 XL160 visible. XL160 had been converted to a K.2 tanker in 1970. Both retired in 1993 and were scrapped. XL160's cockpit was retained and, by 2018, it was back at Marham being showcased in the Aviation Heritage Centre. (Courtesy of RAF Museum)

31 March 1982, with the overly cautious Admiral Terence Lewin in New Zealand on an official visit. Beetham's naval counterpart, the First Sea Lord and Chief of the Navy Staff, Admiral Sir Henry Leach, was at loggerheads with the Defence Secretary, John Nott, who had just proposed radical cuts in the navy's surface fleet and residual airpower, confining it to its NATO role as an anti-submarine force.

Tensions between Britain and Argentina over the disputed Falkland Islands/Malvinas had risen swiftly after Argentinian scrap-metal merchant Constantino Davidoff's commercial venture on the 19th March to dismantle a Leith whaling station on South Georgia Island. Davidoff's salvage workers had been reinforced with a detachment of marines masquerading as civilian scientists commanded by Lieutenant Alfredo Astiz. A British Antarctic Survey field party also there observed a military-style parade where ten Argentinian marines raised the Argentine flag on an electrical tower. In response, on 21 March, HMS *Endurance* sailed from Stanley harbour for South Georgia with 13 Royal Marines reinforced with a detachment of nine from Naval Party 8901, Falklands garrison. *Endurance* reached South Georgia early on 24 March and anchored at Grytviken, 15 miles north of Leith.

With the unease over South Georgia and the Falkland Islands situation, Henry Leach contacted Commander-in-Chief Fleet Admiral Sir John Fieldhouse to ascertain the fleet's state of readiness. 18 Royal Navy destroyers and frigates were participating in NATO Exercise *Spring Train* off Gibraltar. They were commanded from HMS *Antrim* by Rear Admiral John 'Sandy' Woodward, of the First Flotilla. On the 26th March the first Royal Fleet Auxiliary (RFA) ship *Fort Austin* received orders to prepare for deployment to the South Atlantic with the nuclear-powered submarine HMS *Spartan,* which docked in Gibraltar to swap her practice torpedoes for live ones. One of the Royal Navy's two aircraft carriers, HMS *Invincible*, had been sold to the Royal Australian Navy for £175 million and HMS *Hermes* was due to be decommissioned in the autumn of 1982, but Fieldhouse confirmed that *Invincible* and *Hermes* would be brought out of maintenance and crews recalled from leave.

On the evening of the 31st, in Margaret Thatcher's Commons office were people from Whitehall, in a what-to-do meeting of ministers and officials, presided over by the Prime Minister. Not unreasonably, Nott believed there was no way of stopping the imminent Argentinian landing, and that, once made, it would be impossible to reverse it from a starting line 8,000 miles to the north. He saw diplomacy as the only means of limiting the damage. As no British government had ever considered what to do if the Argentinians *did* invade, no military plans existed for such an eventuality. Discussions continued for three-quarters of an hour before the First Sea Lord arrived, still in full uniform from a function at Portsmouth. He pledged that a task force could be mobilized to recapture the islands, despite the distance, and that it could be ready by the weekend. The British armed forces were put on initial alert. For Margaret Thatcher, it was a lifeline.

A last-ditch effort saw Ronald Reagan speak with Leopoldo Galtieri over a conference line from 2034hrs to 2114hrs on 1 April, trying to persuade him not to invade the Falkland Islands. He got nowhere. When pressed whether Argentine military would take action, Galtieri stated that it was an opportune moment unless Britain's government that very night recognized full Argentine sovereignty over all of the Falkland Islands and their dependencies, and agreed to provisions for turning over control within the next few months.[2] Reagan sent a personal message to Prime Minister Margaret Thatcher at 0645Z on 2 April that America had solid information that Argentina was to take military action.

Argentina launched Operation *Rosario* to capture the Falklands on Friday 2 April 1982. Ministry of Defence radio contact with Port Stanley was lost at 0945hrs London (GMT plus 1). Efforts to re-establish communications through HMS *Endurance* began, but by 1300hrs radio contact had not been successful. In the House of Commons the next day – a Saturday, the first weekend sitting since the Suez Crisis of 1956 – the PM was able to galvanize a sense of national loss into one shared purpose, reclaiming

Tanker-to-tanker refuelling over the South Atlantic. Crews of the detachment colloquially known as '112 Multi-Role Victors' were flying an average of 100hrs per month compared to their normal 25hrs pre-conflict. (Courtesy of Brian Armstrong)

the Falkland Islands. The Labour leader Michael Foot's eloquent support in standing up to right-wing military dictators nailed his colours to the flag in backing the Prime Minister. There was a monumental shift, and she consulted Harold Macmillan and others on how to conduct herself. Macmillan advised her to establish a war cabinet.

Defying all doubters the British Cabinet approved the military option on 2 April. In overall command of the British Task Force was Admiral Sir John Fieldhouse, Commander-in-Chief of the Royal Navy, at Fleet Headquarters, in the north-west London suburb of Northwood. Admiral 'Sandy' Woodward had tactical, front-line command of Task Force 317 at sea. Woodward selected HMS *Antrim*, HMS *Glamorgan*, HMS *Coventry*, HMS *Glasgow*, HMS *Sheffield*, HMS *Brilliant*, HMS *Plymouth* and HMS *Arrow* to head south on 2 April. In Britain, at Royal Naval Air Station Yeovilton, 800 Naval Air Squadron left to go onboard HMS *Hermes* for an early departure, and 801 prepared to board HMS *Invincible,* as both aircraft carriers were being made ready for operational deployment, along with all available frigates, destroyers and amphibious warships.

Fieldhouse appointed Air Marshal Sir John Curtiss, co-located at Northwood, his air commander. Initially only a small number of Nimrods and C-130s were viewed as having a role in Task Force 317's mission to the South Atlantic, and five Hercules were dispatched from RAF Lyneham to Gibraltar and Ascension Island with vital supplies for Sandy Woodward's task force. Curtiss also brought in staff and their kit from the Maritime Tactical School based at HMS *Dryad* to act as contingency planners at Northwood.

Ascension

The nearest British-owned staging location was Ascension Island — a 33.9 square mile spit of land 3,900 miles away from the Falklands and another remnant of Britain's empire, but one now used by the Americans. Ascension Island's strategic role had begun after the Napoleonic Wars, when Napoleon was exiled to St Helena to the south-east, and Ascension was garrisoned by the Royal Navy. Over the 19th century it evolved from a victualling and coaling station into a mid-Atlantic communication powerhouse. In December 1899, the Eastern Telegraph Company (ETC) installed the first of an underwater cable network linking Britain with Cape Town, South Africa (1900), then followed it with connections to Freetown in Sierra Leone (1901), and Buenos Aires (1910) through roughly 100,000 miles of cables. ETC merged with Cable & Wireless, and by 1942 its employees were cabling half a million messages every month.

Vulcan XM607 on the apron at Wideawake. A cluster of technicians with ear defenders stand around a Bronze Green Land Rover with its sticks and holes supporting a rolled soft-top roof. Nearby on the left is a 'Palouste' air start unit used to start the engines. On the right-hand side is a ground power unit (GPU), probably a diesel electric set. (Andrew D. Bird Collection)

Despite America's early neutrality in World War II, it was already negotiating with Britain over military bases that would stretch its global reach, with the Destroyers for Bases agreement signed in September 1940. In November 1941, one month before the Japanese attack on the American naval base at Pearl Harbor, the governor of St Helena relayed a classified message to Stephen Cardwell, Cable & Wireless's general manager, instructing him to survey Ascension for a site appropriate for building an airstrip. Already, it was stated that the Americans would be involved.

The airfield at Ascension would be built by the US military, by arrangement with the British government, for airpower was proving a key weapon in the Battle of the Atlantic. Basing long-range aircraft on Ascension would provide air cover over a section of the central Atlantic, as well as enabling US aircraft to transit via Ascension to North Africa and the Mediterranean. A site at Waterloo Plain was proposed for the airfield, which would be named after the numerous sooty terns that inhabited the area, known as 'wideawake birds'. Lieutenant Colonel James Kemp surveyed the site using the Vought OS2U Kingfisher floatplane from the cruiser USS *Omaha*, and concluded the site was excellent.

The task of building Wideawake Field was given to the US Army's 38th Combat Engineer Regiment under the codename Operation *Agate*. The airfield was officially open after 91 days of construction. In World War II, Wideawake had a fuel depot with eight steel tanks for aviation fuel holding 462,000 gallons each, supplied by offshore tankers via a 1,100ft pipeline into Clarence Bay. Two radar stations were built, as was a road system to connect the airfield to Georgetown.

Post-war, in August 1955, President Dwight Eisenhower signed an agreement with Prime Minister Anthony Eden to re-establish a US Air Force base at Wideawake. The Eastern Test Range station was erected in 1957, to track and monitor missiles launched from Cape Canaveral in Florida. A decade later, the Wideawake runway was extended to 10,000ft to meet the demands of the jet age. NASA established a spaceflight tracking and deep space station (DSS 72), operated by the Bendix Field Engineering Corporation, based in Maryland, for the Jet Propulsion Laboratory within the California Institute of Technology at Devil's Ashpit, which supported the Apollo spaceflight programme. Apollo missions were monitored by two 9m AZ-EL-mounted antennae with high angular-tracking rates, while the base's deep-space antenna had a nominal communications range of 60,300km. The location of this installation was separated by Green Mountain, whose peak at 2,819ft meant maximum protection from noise or interference from Cable & Wireless when using the Intel Sat II for Apollo missions. The NASA station at Wideawake was the first to receive perhaps the world's most famous radio transmission: 'The Eagle has landed.'

By 1980 there were 800 permanent residents on the island, most of whom were originally from St Helena. Lieutenant Colonel William Bryden US Air Force (USAF) commanded Ascension Auxiliary Air Force Base and the US tracking station. Known as 'Bill', he was a master navigator who had flown 105 combat missions in the Vietnam War in AC-119K gunships. In 1978 he joined the Test and Evaluation section of the Headquarters Air Force Systems Command at Andrews Air Force Base, Maryland, and held the position of chief of test policy until assuming command on Ascension. Technical and support services for the US air base and tracking station were supplied under contract to the Air Force by 73 Americans from RCA, 63 from Bendix and 31 from Pan American. Around 25 times a month, Pan Am Cargo's Boeing 707-321Cs flew in supplies or rotated contractors monitoring US missile and satellite tracking missions. This pattern remained unaltered for 'Bill' Bryden until a phone call at 0830hrs on 2 April 1982, when a journalist from London's *Evening Standard*

In the foreground there are two Harrier GR.3s of No 1 (F) Squadron, sent to provide air cover for Ascension Island. In their first take-off, both took off vertically rather than use Wideawake's runway and burned a significant hole in the asphalt. American Bill Bryden was forced to limit the runway to 7,000ft for two days while it was resurfaced. (Andrew D. Bird Collection)

queried how many aircraft he expected from the RAF and how far it was from Ascension to the Falkland Islands. He had no idea what she was talking about.

In response to concerns over neutrality, Dean Fischer, Assistant Secretary of State for Public Affairs, advised that:

> Our view on this is that Ascension Island is a British possession. The United Kingdom has the legal right to land military aircraft there after notifying you, the U.S. Air Force Commander, at the airfield. The U.S. Government is obligated under a 1962 agreement governing its use of the airfield, to cooperate in the United Kingdom's use of logistic, administrative, or operating facilities; and therefore, such use of the airfield does not, in any way constitute U.S. involvement in the United Kingdom–Argentine dispute.

Lord Carrington sent a formal notification of the British government's intentions on 2 April through the British Embassy in Washington, advising the US authorities that British forces planned to use Ascension's facilities to support the British airlift operation that was getting underway. He requested the airfield operated on a 24-hour basis which would see Wideawake temporarily becoming the world's busiest operational airfield. Any equipment or ammunition that the warships lacked due to their hasty departure had to be flown to Ascension Island, as did anything the base required to function as the forward logistic support for Operation *Corporate*. The increasing operational tempo saw American JP-5 aviation fuel stocks rapidly diminish: 100,000 gallons of JP-5 had already been consumed by 7 April. The British estimated JP-5 consumption rate at 660,000 to 800,000 gallons per week to support air operations at Ascension. A USAF tanker pumped off 1.3 million gallons on 9 April into US stocks, Washington's British Air Attaché requesting that this offloading 'fill the storage tanks to full capacity for RAF use.' This would meet logistical needs for three weeks. The US Embassy in London informed the Thatcher government that if there was urgent need of JP-5 and, should the US not be able to meet this requirement, they would have no objection to the British delivering additional fuel by means of their own tankers.

An additional request for fuel support by the British arrived on 13 April. Washington's own computations saw a further 900,000 gallons (just over one week's supply) released by the United States on the island. Even with access to this fuel, Washington's British Air Attaché estimated the RAF would run out on approximately 20 April. 250,000 gallons had been consumed by Monday 19 April, and just 12,000 gallons remained by the Thursday, meaning an adjustment to RAF operations to compensate. However, Bryden spoke with the Pentagon, and US Secretary of Defense, Caspar Weinberger, requested the Defense Fuel Supply Center and the Military Sealift Command pull a tanker out of a US exercise in the Caribbean and redirect it to Ascension to replenish Wideawake's fuel tanks with 2.4 million US gallons of JP-5 jet fuel (nearly Wideawake's full capacity of 2.5 million). The tanker was to arrive on

A Victor tanker is dwarfed by a Lockheed Martin Galaxy C-5A (00464) with a USAF C-141 Starlifter (700X) behind. America airlifted crucial missile stocks, including 105 Sidewinder missiles, to the South Atlantic to bolster British air defences. In the foreground is Victor XL189 on the runway; this was Bob Tuxford's aircraft on *Black Buck 1*. (Reproduced by kind permission of Air Mobility Command Museum and National Museum of the US Air Force)

24–25 April. Bryden received orders meanwhile, to draw on US war reserve stock to meet the RAF requirements until the tanker arrived.

The JP-5 was discharged from the tanker at Catherine Point using a floating pipeline and transferred to the tank farm at Georgetown, 3 miles from Wideawake. Fuel was normally pumped into bowsers, but a bottleneck quickly formed, even with an additional 12 Leyland Hippo refuellers, each of 2,500-gallon capacity. The road surface (built from volcanic ash) was abrasive, and soon flat tyres caused further disruption. This was resolved by 1 Troop, 51 (Construction) Squadron Royal Engineers, who laid a 4-mile-long pipeline from the farm to Wideawake to replace the refuelling lorries. An additional 180,000-gallon bulk tank facility, using fuel bladders, was installed at the airfield by the Royal Engineers and operated by 12 Petroleum Operations Section Royal Army Ordnance Corps. By the time military operations ceased in mid-1982, Ascension had transferred six million gallons of aviation fuel from US tankers.

Diplomacy

During the Task Force's voyage south, Margaret Thatcher had both to maintain pressure on Argentina and keep critics and allies satisfied that she was open to a negotiated withdrawal. This was not easy. The new Reagan administration opposed the war, having cultivated good relations with the Galtieri Junta in Argentina in the hope that it would prove an important ally in the battle against Soviet influence in central America. The United States feared that the Junta's fall would bring the return of a left-wing, Peronist government, and it also had significant financial and personal interests in Argentina. As much as one-fifth of US banking capital was exposed if Argentina defaulted on its debt and there were as many as 16,000 Americans resident in the country.

There was no great understanding on Capitol Hill or the US Embassy in London of the depth of the crisis the invasion had provoked in the House of Commons, with near-unanimity across the political spectrum on the need for military action. In America, the State Department saw the conflict as a throwback to Britain's imperial past, and Jeane Kirkpatrick, the US Ambassador to the UN and a Cabinet member, made little or no effort to disguise her distaste for American diplomatic support of Britain. She thought a policy of neutrality made sense from the point of view of US interests and would do Britain no harm, but she was far from passive. Reagan's Secretary of State, Alexander Haig, tried unsuccessfully to act as mediator, flying to both London and Buenos Aires. There was probably little chance of success, but his efforts were seriously undermined by the undisguised support offered to Argentina by Kirkpatrick, who held regular contacts with members of the Galtieri government to pass on details of her government's latest diplomatic intentions. Kirkpatrick also had grave concerns about the implications of the Rio Treaty. Latin Americans were lining up behind Argentina and the whole hemisphere could become involved. Reagan hoped to retain the friendship of all of Latin America, but it was more important that Britain did not fail. Anglophile Caspar Weinberger's Department of Defense began a number of non-public actions of substantial covert support while outwardly portraying itself as neutral, before America came down politically on the side of Thatcher and Britain.

Economic sanctions began on 6 April. Embargos on military kit going to Argentina saw $6–7 million of American spares in the pipeline halted. European sanctions were of greater military significance: French aircraft and missiles (underway) were embargoed by President Mitterrand, but a clear breach saw a French technical team of Dassault stay in Argentina.[3] In Paris, Ambassador Gerardo Schamis, Argentine Ambassador to France, spoke with American Ambassador-at-Large, Vernon Walters, whom he had known for many years, and indicated a British Task Force had sailed. Schamis flashed an urgent signal to the Argentine Foreign Ministry but Nicanor Costa Méndez ignored his message, believing that the US was in a position to achieve a satisfactory solution before the British reached the 50th or 40th parallel. Options for resolving the Falklands dispute meant Secretary of State, Alexander Haig, continued lengthy and intensive discussions.

Vulcan XM598 touching back down on Ascension's Wideawake. (Crown Copyright MOD)

Haig was seriously concerned that Thatcher had been listening largely to the Ministry of Defence, especially senior naval and air force officers, and might not have adequately considered non-military options. At the end of April, Haig produced terms of a settlement, a very reasonable proposal, which safeguarded British sovereignty but left open the possibility of negotiating at some stage. The Argentinians rejected it, and the PM's Cabinet never had to reply to his proposal. Haig took this rejection by Galtieri as a contributing factor to the Reagan administration coming down on Britain's side. The failure to avert the conflict ultimately cost Haig his job as Secretary of State.

The Vulcans

After his initial Commons meeting with the Prime Minister and Henry Leach, Air Chief Marshal Michael Beetham realized that the conflict would require massive transport and strategic tanker support immediately and put squadrons on standby. The discussion with the Air Staff of what the Royal Air Force could do with the resources available was more challenging. There was speculation in the British and American press that the delta-wing Avro Vulcan bomber, conceived in the reign of George VI, might be used to target Argentina and the Falkland Islands, which was not actively discouraged by the newly formed War Cabinet. Ironically, one of the first stunts which showed the Vulcan's ability to fly a great distance (albeit with refuelling stops) was a flight to Argentina's capital Buenos Aires in 1958. Dr Arturo Frondizi had become the first elected Argentine president in 12 years and on 1 May 1958 two B.1 nuclear bombers entered Argentinian airspace for an airborne salute over the inauguration ceremony.

Just over 20 years later, the RAF's last three Vulcan squadrons, Nos 44, 50 and 101, were preparing to be disbanded on 30 June, with the remaining aircraft sent to aviation museums or scrapyards. Beetham reached back to this technology believing that the Vulcan could contribute to the retaking of the Islands; however, there was an immediate realization that the RAF simply did not have the right kit for an adventure in the South Atlantic. The Vulcan was the longest-range bomber that the RAF possessed, able to fly 2,600 miles at 50,000ft. Unfortunately Ascension Island, the closest available airfield to the Falklands, was an 8,000-mile round trip away.

---

3   Team's leader, Herve Colin, admitted carrying out one Exocet missile test that proved invaluable to Argentinian forces to determine if the missile launcher was functioning correctly or not. Three launches failed; the team located the source of the problem and the Argentinians were able to fire Exocets at the Task Force using three previously faulty missile launchers which they fitted to under wing pylons.

Avro Vulcan showing the cockpit pressure dome (yellow) with the central scanner bay hatch from the cabin, as well as the internal refuelling supply pipe, mount and the wiring. The dome would also house the radar mount and HS2 radar unit and the rotating radar scanner. If the HS2 scanner toppled or was unusable in flight, to stop it bumping around, the radar navigator would crawl to insert a key and fix it upright fore and aft to stop rotation. (Anthony Wright)

RAF Waddington was the only remaining Vulcan base, where Group Captain John Laycock, the base commander, received his orders on Good Friday, 9 April. He recalled from Easter leave his next-door neighbour, Wing Commander Simon Baldwin, the commanding officer of No. 44 Squadron, to head up the Vulcan effort in the Falklands. His remit was to integrate a team drawn from the Waddington Operations Wing planning staff and the remaining Vulcan squadrons. The base's conference room was utilized as the hub with extra telephones installed and Baldwin's team set about planning what were the longest-range bombing missions in the history of air warfare, and would remain so until October 2001 when a USAF B-2 flew a mission of 44.3hrs to Afghanistan and back from Whiteman Air Force Base in Missouri.

Selecting and refitting the aircraft

Not all of the ageing fleet of Vulcans were fit for the extremes that a Falklands raid would involve. It was deemed essential for *Black Buck* Vulcans to have the more powerful Rolls-Royce Olympus 301 turbojets, giving 20,000lb (88.96kN) of thrust compared to 17,000lb from the 201 series. From the 36 Vulcans that remained operational, 18 were equipped with the Olympus 301s, and to extend the lifespan of each engine they had been flown more gently, to a maximum of 97.5 per cent of full thrust. From this shortlist, selecting airframes meant checking their fatigue meter, which monitored the g-forces the airframe was subjected to during each sortie. At each predetermined interval on the meter, the aircraft would have the appropriate maintenance carried out by the manufacturers, and would be then returned with an effective zero rating. Those airframes with a high fatigue count were removed from the equation.

The standard of instrumentation also varied among aircraft, and those with the best analogue bombing computers were selected. Each mechanical device had particular characteristics, and some performed better than others. Technicians examined the computers' performance results and reduced the pool of Vulcans from 18 to six: serial XL391; XM597; XM598; XM607; XM612; and XM654. Waddington then had to add an additional electronic countermeasures (ECM) device, as although the onboard jamming systems were effective against legacy Soviet equipment, they were ineffective against emerging threats and the modern Western-made systems used by Argentina. The solution utilized an AN/ALQ-101D (or 'Dash 10') jamming pod, as fitted on the RAF's Buccaneer force, integrated onto the aircraft using the hardpoints originally intended for the Douglas GAM-87A Skybolt air-launched nuclear ballistic missiles, which were made redundant when Britain signed up for Polaris in 1962. These Vulcans received a beefed-up outer wing structure with a hardpoint and necessary wiring for a Skybolt pylon, with updates to the navigation system as the aircraft was incompatible with the missile. These modifications could be made to Vulcans that were in production, with 60 existing B.2s being returned to Avro for conversion. The intention was to have 72 Vulcan B.2 variants for 140 Skybolt missiles.

Not all paper-based aircraft records had been transferred on to the new RAF computer system by April 1982. Therefore the Waddington engineering team did not know which of the individual Vulcans that remained in service had the full fore and aft Skybolt missile attachments and associated ducting that would be required for the new cabling necessary for

RAF Avro Vulcan B.2 possibles for *Black Buck* operations				
Aircraft serial no.	Olympus 301s[1]	Full Skybolt	Partial Skybolt	Black Buck op
XH557	•		•	
XJ748	•		•	
XL386	•			
XL391[2]	•	•		•
XM575	•			
XM594	•			
XM597	•	•		•
XM598	•	•		•
XM606	•			
XM607	•	•		•
XM612	•	•		•
XM647	•		•	
XM648	•		•	
XM651	•		•	
XM652	•		•	
XM654[3]	•		•	•
XM655	•		•	
XM656	•		•	
Total: 38	18	5	9	6

1. 18 Avro Vulcan B.2s fitted with Olympus 201s were on strength at RAF Waddington: XH558*, XH560*, XH561*, XH562*, XJ783*, XJ823*, XJ825*, XL319, XL321, XL360, XL426, XL444, XL445, XM569, XM571, XM527, XM573. Those marked with * had only partial Skybolt modifications.
2. XL391 was not equipped with the X-band jammer normally fitted in front of the ECM bay inspection door in the rear fuselage; it stayed at RAF Waddington in reserve.
3. XM654 was partially brought up to *Black Buck* specification, and kept at RAF Waddington as a reserve.

carrying external stores. In some cases they were totally absent during external checks, while five different permutations for external underwing attachments were recorded.

Those equipped with the appropriate combination to carry the Skybolt consisted of a twin forward attachment point, a single one to the rear and a small blister or fairing situated immediately ahead of the forward attachment points. The blister was originally intended to provide the Skybolt with coolant but for *Black Buck* it was to be utilized to feed the wiring loom through the wing to the cockpit. Inspecting XM654, the appropriate combination was not seen, while XM606 had a low fatigue life remaining so was discounted. No manufacturing plans for the Vulcan pylons were located at either British Aerospace Systems nor the RAF Museum in London, so the engineering team at Waddington had to design and manufacture the hardpoints. Each was individually constructed using material from a hardware store.

The remaining five – XL391, XM597, XM598, XM607 and XM612

Avro Vulcan B.2 assembly line at the factory site at Woodford which had undergone expansion to accommodate the Vulcan. Some 136 aircraft were built (45 to the B.1 design and 89 B.2 models) with B.2's XM597, XM598 and XM607 reaching notoriety during the Falkland Crisis in 1982, some 26 years after the first flight. (Andrew D. Bird Collection)

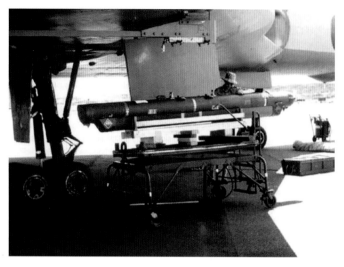

The Vulcans' self-defence was improved by the addition of the AN/ALQ-101 or Dash-10 pod used to counter radar-guided weapons, purloined from Buccaneers based at RAF Honington. This ECM equipment was critical on *Black Buck* sorties when penetrating the Argentine radar defences. (Crown Copyright MOD)

– had all the full specifications, but still required attention. Their Olympus 301s had to be restored to full thrust, and the long over-water flight meant that the Vulcans' traditional method of radar navigation using ground features was not an option. Astronavigation was too inaccurate for a mission that demanded precision navigation. Instead, the Delco Carousel inertial navigation system, sourced from British Airways supplies or scavenged from ex-British Airways Super VC-10 jet airliners awaiting conversion into tankers at RAF Abingdon and RAF Brize Norton, provided increased navigation accuracy for both Vulcans and Victors over the large expanse of the South Atlantic Ocean.

With the Vulcans limited to an operational range of 2,607 miles, air-to-air refuelling would be essential. However, missions had lapsed in the post-Polaris years and with the contraction of deployments globally, no Vulcan pilots were current in air-to-air refuelling – in fact it had been 13 years since a Vulcan had even undertaken this task, which the bomber crews had been led to believe was the strict preserve of intensely trained fighter pilots.

It was not merely training that had to be refreshed – the Vulcans' technical capability to conduct air-to-air refuelling had to be renewed. Engineers replaced their 4in non-return valves, thanks to 20 replacements that were located on a shelf at RAF Stafford. By Easter Monday, 11 April, engineers had rebuilt a serviceable in-flight refuelling system after dried-out seals were replaced, pipes checked under pressure for leaks and corrosion on the probe nozzle remedied, while one crucial component was discovered in the engineers' mess, serving as an ashtray! More kit was reclaimed from airframes in Britain and America: the vital bomb carriers to hitch iron bombs inside the bomb bay. Likewise, the nuclear weapon release panel had been replaced by the 90-way selector panel for greater accuracy in bombing competitions, which worked by enabling three offset points to be used during the run. None could be located on the RAF computer system, but boxes of them were rescued from a skip at RAF Scampton.

Four Vulcans that had been configured for nuclear missions, XM597, XM598, XM607 and XM612, were thus converted back to the conventional bombing role, then had their individual squadron markings blanked out and the underside resprayed in Dark Sea Grey. Calibrated to tolerances specified in the aircraft manual, they were signed off as up to standard, backed by ample stocks of engines and spares. However, there was also a major logistical problem in getting an adequate supply of ordnance to Ascension. The solution would be to load the bombs prior to flying to the islands; although bombers do not usually fly and land with a full bomb load, these were exceptional circumstances. Vulcan XM564 was partially brought up to operational level, and XL391 became a second reserve. As the RAF hastily regenerated its air-to-air refuelling capabilities, other aircraft required attention – the remaining Vulcans were cannibalized for their fuelling probes and systems. Curtiss extended mid-air refuelling capability with the conversion of C-130s and the Nimrods, allowing them to take their Searchwater radar much farther south than their original 1,800-mile range. So sophisticated was the Nimrods' radar that they could distinguish between submarines and whales – a problem that haunted the Task Force as it steamed south, watching for Argentine attack but coincidentally also following the mammals' southward migration.

Aircrews and training

On the morning of Easter Monday four senior officers met at Waddington to select crews. Flight Lieutenant Martin Withers and Squadron Leader Alastair 'Monty' Montgomery were recently back from *Red Flag,* a yearly US war game exercise over the deserts of the US southwest. Both were experienced in flying formation which would be required for air-to-air refuelling. Squadron Leader Neil McDougall had not been deployed to Nevada with Montgomery and Withers, but had more experience as he was the only one on base who had flown on air-refuelling sorties, albeit back in the 1960s when the tanker was a Vickers Valiant. However, RAF Marham's stretched tanker resources meant that only three crews could be supported so McDougall became the reserve and was replaced by Squadron Leader John Reeve.

Three air-to-air refuelling instructors (AARIs) arrived at Waddington. Flight Lieutenants Dick Russell, Pete Standing and Ian Clifford, well-practised in the manoeuvre, were to teach both the Vulcan pilots and co-pilots. After each crew had a brief simulator experience, airborne refuelling training for real began on 13 April, and each crew was to complete three mid-air 'prods', one by day and two at night. Time constraints meant that only the pilots and not the co-pilots were trained, and on 27 April Russell and the two other AARIs were told they would be joining the Vulcan crews on the mission itself. During the work-up to perform this task, the day and night tanker training was cut short when the assigned Victors of No. 55 and No. 57 Squadron were redeployed to Ascension.

Air Vice-Marshal Mike Knight's decision that the AARIs should fly the mission meant an adjustment to the V-bomber crews' cohesive units. The AARI would sit in the co-pilot's right-hand seat then either fly or supervise 'prods' on the flight until the bomb run. The Vulcan co-pilot sat in a jump seat in the crew compartment. After the final 'prod' the air electronics officer would help them swap places by disarming the co-pilot's ejector seat, after which the AARI unstrapped himself, squeezed between the seats and went down the ladder. The co-pilot would then climb up the ladder onto the flight deck to join his captain. The reverse took place for the return leg. The arrangement was quickly grasped as it relieved the strain on the pilot, who needed to focus on the run into the target, and added a reserve if either pilot or co-pilot was incapacitated.

The pressure from Air Commander John Curtiss to get them to Ascension and into the theatre of operations was immense. Simon Baldwin ramped up the training schedule, with each crew clocking 50hrs in ten days, of which 70 per cent was at night. The refuelling valves had to be modified to achieve connections without fuel leaking over the Vulcans' windscreens. After disassembling the valves, the technicians identified a modification that had been made on the Victors' refuelling valves but not implemented on the Vulcans', as the system was redundant. The modification did the trick late on 26 April, and Reeve, Withers and Montgomery successfully completed their air refuelling conversion.

The crews flew simulated missions with their bomb bay holding seven 1,000lb iron bombs armed with nose and tail fusing; with no delayed fuses they would detonate instantly on hitting the Ministry of Defence bombing range at Garvie Island, off Cape Wrath in the far north-west of Scotland. Ewes were lambing at Balnakeil near Cape Wrath, and the nearby crofters and farmers received an emergency warning from the Highland regional authorities that the Vulcans would be operating during the lambing season. Compensation was offered by the Ministry of Defence if ewes miscarried.

On 20 April the three Vulcans conducted a low-level training operation at Cape Wrath. At 350ft the navigation

Avro Vulcan B.2 XM607 when back at Waddington with bomb tally markings for successful missions targeting Port Stanley airport runway, as follows: 30 April–1 May Flight Lieutenant Martin Withers; 3–4 May Squadron Leader John Reeve; 12 June Flight Lieutenant Martin Withers.

Avro Vulcan bomb bay looking towards the rear of the aircraft showing the 'Vulcan Seven Store Carrier' which was suspended holding seven 1,000lb conventional high explosive (HE) bombs. (Andrew D. Bird Collection)

radar operators in the back of the aircraft spoke to the pilots to correct for drift while the pilots on the flight deck kept the Vulcan straight and level. The bomb run had to be conducted without any adjustments in speed, otherwise as the bombs separated from their racks the strike pattern would be affected, so fine were the margins. When the 1,000lb bombs dropped, each deployed a small parachute from the tail cone to slow its descent, to ensure that the Vulcan had enough time to escape from the detonation. It was challenging for all, and rather disappointing for the navigation radar operators, who were becoming familiar with conventional arming and release procedures on the bomber's old analogue computers, to find that having released their bomb load they would see it drift downwind and fall harmlessly into the sea instead of producing a fierce hail of iron and rock. Before returning to Waddington the trio set off down the Scottish west coast before tearing over the border into Cumbria to their target – RAF Spadeadam, or 'Spadeadam Waste', a huge electronic warfare range whose staff had hastily reprogrammed computer systems to replicate the emissions of the fire-control radars and the surface-to-air missiles known to be operated by the Argentines. The Dash-10 jamming pod worked by picking up the detection pulse of the enemy fire-control radar and electronically altered the radar return of the incoming jet to place it in airspace four or five miles away.

Target

Air Vice-Marshal Ken Hayr, the officer tasked to manage the formidable air operations in the South Atlantic, purloined drawings of the Port Stanley airport runway specifications, which showed that the layers comprised a minimum of 32mm of asphalt surface, then 300mm of compacted crushed stone, then white sand underneath. A single airport terminal building and parking apron had also been built, in addition to a number of smaller storage buildings. Hayr's briefing for Sir Michael Beetham had seen him chew over the difficulties of hitting mainland Argentina, which was legally questionable, politically provocative and not worth the fallout. He arrived at the same conclusion as Baldwin: that the Port Stanley runway, on a spur of land next to the coast and running almost east–west, appeared to be the only viable military target for the Vulcans' bombs. The mission would impede Argentina's ability to wield air power from Port Stanley airfield, and thus support the Royal Navy's approach and the eventual amphibious landings, which would be codenamed Operation *Sutton*.

Beetham was instrumental in getting the mission approved by the Chiefs of the Defence Staff and told John Nott that the mission was militarily feasible with a good chance of success. The bombing runs over the Cape Wrath range showed that seven 1,000lb bombs were not enough, but a full load of 21 would do the job. If dropped at low level on the Stanley runway, there would be a 90 per cent probability that this would cause one crater and a 75 per cent chance of inflicting two. Air Vice-Marshal Mike Knight's planning team at No. 1 Group, RAF Bawtry, and Simon Baldwin at RAF Waddington knew that the enemy had anti-aircraft artillery (AAA) and surface-to-air missiles (SAMs) around Stanley, and air defence radars, so they changed the height of the bomb run. The Roland SAM was the main threat, effective up to 16,000ft, but intelligence said these had not been deployed. A bomb run at 8,000ft-plus was an acceptable attack height. It did not completely remove the dangers, but the plan meant a low-level approach under Argentinian radar; pop up to 8,000ft or above; use the ECMs to blind the Argentine radar; release the free-fall 1,000lb bombs, with enough spacing, to achieve a 35-degree runway cut. At least one of the bombs should hit the target, and the element of surprise would give the Argentinians only seconds to react, meaning that in theory the attacking Vulcans should be safe from threats based in Port Stanley, including any Argentinian fighters in the Falklands, and also that they were unlikely to be intercepted by jets from the mainland. Waddington's base commander John Laycock gave it his approval, and the crews practised the new mission profile twice, as the political debate over the use of RAF bombers in the war continued. The Prime Minister and Defence Secretary John Nott were positive about the deployment of Vulcans to the Ascension Islands, while Foreign Secretary Francis Pym and Deputy Prime Minister William Whitelaw had doubts. Pym had been named Foreign Secretary after the resignation of Lord Carrington on 5 April. Pym and Whitelaw were uncomfortable with the implications of military action and were left increasingly isolated, with Pym having suggested previously that the recapture of South Georgia by Argentine Marines had created a new opportunity for settlement, on a kind of 'honours even' basis. Margaret Thatcher did not see things that way, and the deployment was authorized on 27 April.

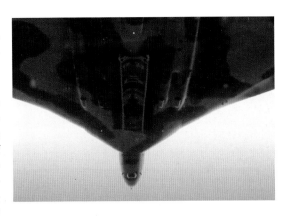

A still photograph taken from a camera mount on the underside of an Avro Vulcan showing an open bomb bay after dropping practice bombs off the coast of Scotland. (Andrew D. Bird Collection)

The Victors and Nimrods

All *Black Buck* missions were entirely dependent upon the RAF's support aircraft for their long-range operations. It had been a good decision for the Ministry of Defence to convert Handley-Page Victor B.2 bombers into K.2 tankers,[4] although the original order for 29 K.2 tankers was reduced in February 1975 to 24 aircraft. In 1982 most of these were on the strength of either No. 55 or No. 57 Squadron at RAF Marham.

The tanker conversion programme, carried out at British Aerospace Woodford, involved not only the installation of refuelling equipment but also a renewal of each aircraft's fatigue life. Thirty-two separate tanks were fitted, so that the tanker could pump fuel from any one of them to another to maintain the aircraft's centre of gravity. The total fuel capacity was to be 128,000lb, with 67,000lb contained in 16 separate tanks positioned in every space available in the length of the fuselage, and two massive tanks in the former bomb bay. The internal wing space contained 32,000lb, spread among 12 tanks, and the large underwing tanks contained a further 27,000lb. Each wingtip tank provided an additional 1,000lb of fuel capacity. To give it some perspective, the underground fuel storage below a roadside petrol station holds fuel in the region of 46,000lb (22,000 litres), depending on the number of pumps. In-flight fuel was transferred from the port wing group and forward bomb bay tank which normally supplied the port Mk.20 refuelling pod, while the starboard wing group and aft bomb bay tank supplied the starboard Mk.20 pod.

Since May 1978, when the final Victor XH672 was delivered and joined No. 57 Squadron at RAF Marham, the tanker crews had continuously performed in their peacetime role, refuelling British and allied fighters, predominantly RAF interceptors from the Quick Reaction Alert (QRA) units. These fighters scrambled from east-coast air bases to intercept long-range Russian aircraft over the North Sea, and were supported by air-to-air refuelling aircraft. This role routinely tested the RAF's reactions, and both fighters and tankers had to be able to respond to an airborne threat 24 hours a day, 365 days a year. This experience

---

4   The conversions had been authorized by Edward, Baron Shackleton, who had been Minister of Defence for the RAF between 1964 and 1967, and who would later research and write the 1977 Falklands Report.

would be key to the conduct of air offensives during Operation *Corporate*, although long-range flights over the unfamiliar South Atlantic Ocean necessitated upgrades to the Victors' navigational equipment, notably the installation of the Delco Carousel inertial navigation system and the Omega navigation system.

Air Marshal Sir John Curtiss, Air Officer Commanding the RAF's maritime group, No. 18 Group, learned that none of the ten Victor K.2 crews of No. 55 Squadron or No. 57 Squadron selected for deployment were trained in night receiver techniques (i.e. capable of taking on fuel from another tanker in darkness), as it had been deemed unnecessary. However, K.1 pilots were qualified to do so, so each K.2 had an experienced former K.1 pilot assigned, after which the crew underwent night air-to-air refuelling training with an instructor over two nights to qualify ready for deployment on 18 April. Preparations complete, RAF personnel from Marham deployed in mid-April to Ascension Island. The ground crew technician and engineers were drawn from the Vulcan squadrons at Waddington to form No. 195 (A) Squadron, a composite squadron whose task was to maintain the Vulcans used in operations.

The second RAF asset deployed to Ascension was its maritime patrol aircraft, the Hawker-Siddeley Nimrod. This was a design that dated back to the dawn of the jet era, based on an extensive modification of the De Havilland Comet, the world's first jet airliner which first flew in 1949. The Nimrod was introduced to RAF squadrons in October 1969 and designated MR.1. By 1975, 35 of the original 45 aircraft had been taken out of service and modernized with a new electronic suite, and designated MR.2.

Based at either RAF St Mawgan in Cornwall or RAF Kinloss in north-east Scotland, the Nimrods' operations varied from hunting Soviet submarines to maritime search-and-rescue. Shortly before deploying to the South Atlantic, a Nimrod coordinated the rescue by helicopters of survivors from MV *Manchester* and MV *Victory* south-west of Cornwall. On 5 April, No. 42 Squadron's Wing Commander Davie Bough received a signal to deploy MR.1s to Ascension in support of the Task Force. Both versions of the aircraft, which was designed for anti-submarine duties, with a crew of 14, and equipped with a bomb bay and wing pylons to mount a variety of weapons, would play a vital role in securing the Falkland Islands. Nimrods XV244 and XV258 flew out first, but as neither had in-flight refuelling probes they were routed via Gibraltar to Ascension Island, and arrived on 6 April. It was imperative for the Nimrod fleet to be modified to support air-to-air refuelling. John Scott-Wilson at BAe Manchester estimated that it would take one month to design, fit and clear air-to-air refuelling systems.

An Avro Vulcan at RAF Waddington prior to repainting, with a Martel missile attached on the port side, and a Dash-10 jammer on the starboard side. (Crown Copyright MOD)

By 14 April, John Nott had given clearance for Scott-Wilson to proceed and immediately moved his team to Woodford where Nimrod XV229 was ready for modification. Nearby was Vulcan XA603, newly purchased for static display in the proposed Avro Heritage Centre. Within hours the airframe was minus its probe. A metal pipe was then fed through the Nimrod's upper escape hatch, aft of the pilot and co-pilot's seats, which splayed out into two standard fuel bowser hoses secured to the floor with jubilee clips. These ran the length of the aircraft behind the operators' seats to disappear underneath the cabin floor (the engineers having dispensed with a pair of flare chutes) for them to join the aircraft's normal fuel system. This improvised system affected the aircraft's directional stability, so a quick fix saw a wooden keel riveted on under the rear fuselage replacing the standard tail 'bumper', while a vertical avionics antenna, borrowed from the intelligence-gathering Nimrod R.1 variant, was fitted to the top and bottom surfaces of each tailplane to improve aerodynamic stability. With the problem solved, a live transfer of fuel with a Marham Victor was successful on 30 April, and the following day Nimrod XV238 was delivered. Further Nimrods were modified at two sites using fuel probes from Vulcans not selected to participate in Operation *Black Buck*, or which were acting as reserve aircraft. Eighteen pilots then completed air-to-air refuelling instruction for night and day prods and gained rapid qualification. On 7 May a crew then flew the first R.2 XV227 to Ascension, having been refuelled en route.

Commanders based in Britain and on Ascension Island wore multiple hats. The overall commander of Operation *Corporate*, Admiral John Fieldhouse, effectively had control over aviation elements as well, both naval and RAF. Air Vice-Marshal George Chesworth, a veteran maritime pilot with extensive experience in the Korean War and strong leadership qualities, served under Curtiss as the chief of staff of No. 18 Group at Northwood headquarters. Chesworth would be deployed forward to Ascension, making him one of the most important figures in the *Black Buck* missions; he exercised tactical control over air-to-air refuelling and anti-submarine/surveillance aircraft, though the Victors and Nimrods remained under the detachment commanders, respectively Wing Commander David Maurice-Jones and his replacement, Wing Commander Alan Bowman of No. 57 Squadron, and Wing Commander David Emmerson. Chesworth had completed more than 50 missions during the Korean War, including some in extreme conditions, and then had a long and distinguished career as a maritime patrol pilot and commander; he wrote the Air Staff requirement that produced the Nimrod, and commanded the first Nimrod squadron. No jingoistic war lover, Chesworth was described by one of his staff as 'a wise leader and a perfect gentleman' and had a wide

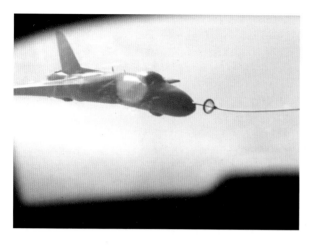

An unidentified Avro Vulcan is lined up to 'prod' the drogue of a Victor to receive fuel. (Andrew D. Bird Collection)

The Anglo-French Martel AS.37 ARM missile attached to the DIY pylon made of quarter-inch-thick steel plate welded into a box section by the technicians at RAF Waddington. (Crown Copyright MOD)

reverence for life, not only for the lives of those serving on Ascension or with the Task Force but also for the enemy's.

Wing Commander David Emmerson, commanding No. 206 Squadron which flew Nimrod MR.2s out of RAF Kinloss, had been briefed on 21 April at the Joint Headquarters at Northwood to take charge of the Nimrod MR.2 deployment on Ascension Island. They would be replacing the Nimrod MR.1s from No. 42 Squadron, XV244 and XV258, which had arrived on 6 April and formed the first permanent detachment on Ascension. The MR.1's deployment coincided with the request to operate on a 24-hour basis, and involved the provision by the US to provide additional air controllers for the two Nimrod aircraft around the clock for an indefinite period (since the missions would be coordinated with naval submarines and the task force). Emmerson had been rapidly cleared to use the brand-new and secret Stingray torpedo, having dropped them on the range at Machrihanish off the Scottish coast. The first MR.2 to arrive was the non-probe-equipped XV230 on 13 April; then four days later XV255 arrived from Kinloss. With the arrival of Nimrod XV227, Emmerson went through a work-up to make crews ready for missions 300 miles off the Argentinian coast and within range of their fighters and spy planes. An encounter by one MR.2 crew with a Boeing TC-92 reconnaissance jet on 12 May prompted the quick installation of two pylons under the wings of the Nimrods to carry AIM 9L air-to-air missiles. The missiles were requested on 14 May by the British Embassy in Washington, and 50–80 missiles were delivered from Naval Weapons Station Charleston to Britain within 24 hours. The Nimrods were rotated back for fitting out. In an audacious move David Emmerson flew Nimrod XV227 to within 60 miles of Argentina, below radar coverage, turning to fly north-east parallel to the Argentine coastline, its Searchwater radar surveying an area 400 miles wide and 1,000 miles long.

Nimrod crews could also pick up signals from No. 51 Squadron's top-secret intelligence-gathering Nimrod R.1. This single jet, XW664 from RAF Wyton, routed out on 5 May, the day after HMS *Sheffield* was hit, via Bermuda and Belize to San Félix Island, a small rock in the Pacific Ocean 600 miles west of the South American coast. On their sorties over the Pacific Ocean, the 29 crew on board harvested valuable intelligence, monitoring activity at Argentina's southern radar, air and naval bases. Intercepts were occasionally communicated to Emmerson's crews before 19 May when Operation *ACME* was closed down by Assistant Chief of the Air Staff, Ken Hayr, because of the risk of the XW664 missions being discovered, despite a request from Woodward for further missions prior to Operation *Sutton*.

Ordnance

Missiles

The only weapons available for a runway strike were British-made conventional unguided 'iron' bombs. For raids against the Argentinian radars, the other high-value target on the Falklands, the Anglo-French AS.37 Martel missile (already in service with the RAF) was initially an option.

A Victor tanker was chosen for a trial fit of the AS.37 on its starboard pylon before deployment, and Vulcan XM597 was trialled with a single AS.37 missile fitted on the port wing pylon for flight and live-fired once on the Aberporth range in Wales. The trial proved that the Martel was a fearsome weapon, if not a predictable one. It had been intended that the missile would fall into the sea short of the target, with the motor firing for only a couple of seconds after launch. It did not go as intended. Its motor fired for a short duration and the missile was propelled towards the target – and locked on. It became such a threat that the radar had to be rapidly switched off and the range hut vacated. The Martel impacted the beach and drove a furrow just short of the hut where the target radar was located. With civilians in close proximity to the targets, the risk of collateral damage was uncomfortably high, given that the Martel had a probability kill (pK) of only 60 per cent, and that its very large 330lb high-explosive warhead would be careering towards Stanley at a speed of Mach 2.

AS.37 Martel missile. Anglo-French passive radar anti-radiation missile version (not used)	
Mass	550kg (1,210lb)
Length	4.18m (13ft 9in)
Diameter	0.4m (16in)
Warhead	150kg (330lb) and fitted with a Misznay-Schardin plate
Detonation mechanism	proximity fuse
Engine	two stage solid propellant rocket motors
Wingspan	1.2m (3 ft 11in)
Operational range	60km (37 miles) max (estimated, and depending on the launch conditions)
Maximum speed	Mach 0.9 +
Guidance system	passive radar homing, video guided

The Martel option would be discontinued by Northwood after *Black Buck 3*, the first (cancelled) attempt to use the weapon in combat. The Martel's role would be taken by the more capable American AGM-45 Shrike missile when this was offered, and once initial avionics problems had been overcome.

AGM-45A Shrike missile	
Mass	390lb (177.06kg)
Length	10ft (3.05m)
Diameter	8in (203mm)
Warhead	67.5kg (149lb) MK 5 MOD 1 (or MK 86 MOD 1) blast-fragmentation, or 66.6kg (147lb) WAU-9/B blast-fragmentation
Wingspan	3ft (914mm)
Operational range	16km AGM-45A, 0km AGM-45B
Maximum speed	Mach 1.5
Guidance system	passive radar homing

GBU-16 Paveway II	
Mass	1,000lb (453kg)
Length	12ft (3.07m)
Diameter	14in (360mm)
Warhead	Mk 83 United States 1,000lb (450kg) HE with Mk 83/BLU-110B/B warhead used with GBU-16 Paveway II
Operational range	14.8km (9.2 miles)
Guidance system	semi-active-laser

AGM-45 Shrike missiles being prepared for transportation by US Air Force personnel. (US National Archives)

1,000lb general-purpose (GP) bomb

Although air power technology had moved into the era of guided weaponry, in January 1982 an estimated 200 1,000lb bombs remained in stock with a manufacturing date of *c*.1955. Remarkably, these would be the only weapons available to target the Port Stanley runway.

Specifications	
Mass	1,000lb (450kg)
Length	119.49in (3,000mm)
Diameter	14.06in (357mm)
Casing	foundry cast or machined
Filling	Tritonal (mixture of 80% TNT and 20% aluminium powder) Torpex (42% RDX, (Research Department explosive) or hexogen) 40% TNT and 18% powdered aluminium)

DEFENDER'S CAPABILITIES
Argentinian forces in the South Atlantic

The Islas Malvinas dispute was not Argentina's only territorial quarrel. Argentina had almost fought with Chile over the islands and demarcation line in the Beagle Channel, the only inland alternative to the Strait of Magellan for passages between the Atlantic and Pacific oceans. Argentina had suffered the humiliation of defeat by arbitration in 1977 when the International Committee of Jurists, a body commissioned by the British Crown – the agreed mediator since 1902 – had found in favour of Chile, whereupon Chile gained a larger stake in the South Atlantic and Antarctica. Although the rights over the area would be renegotiated when the Antarctic Treaty expired in 1991, to have an Argentinian administration comfortably installed in the Islas Malvinas at that point would likely be beneficial. While the national attachment to the islands was longstanding and heartfelt, a successful outcome to Operation *Rosario* would also offer practical advantages.

On 15 December 1981 Vice Admiral Juan Lombardo became Chief of Naval Operations, based at Puerto Belgrano, south-west of Buenos Aires. He reported to Admiral Jorge Anaya, the naval member of the three-man military Junta with Galtieri and Brigadier General Basilio Lami Dozo. During his time as fleet commander, Lombardo had seen 50 Argentinian 'military scientists' set up a base on South Thule, with British Prime Minister James Callaghan agreeing to non-interference. He then began a scheme to restore administration of the islands to Buenos Aires, to coincide with the 150th anniversary of the day when the captain of HMS *Clio* ordered the removal of the Buenos Aires-appointed governor in Port Stanley.

Understandably the Junta thought it a good moment to dust off a plan to seize the Falklands and its dependency, South Georgia. Keen to cleanse the Junta's image after the tortures and killings of the dirty war, Anaya ordered Lombardo to prepare invasion plans to establish Argentine sovereignty of the Islas Malvinas, and also to include a withdrawal plan because the prospect of occupying the islands long-term was not attractive. He estimated it would probably require two weeks to remove the Argentine armed forces. The operation was to involve the Argentinian Air Force, Army, Navy, Marines and Naval Air Arm; but, Lombardo was only to consult with Rear Admiral Carlos Büsser of the Marines, Garcia Bol

The French Super Étendard 3-A-210 Fighter-Bomber was used throughout the Falklands war by Argentinian forces. (Luis Rosendo/Heritage Images via Getty Images)

OPPOSITE THE ATLANTIC OCEAN THEATRE, 1982

of the Naval Air Arm and Captain Gualter Allara, Deputy Foreign Minister. Lombardo struggled to bring all the elements together, and eventually Army General Osvaldo Garcia and Brigadier Sigfrido Plessel of the Air Force joined his planning team; but it nevertheless became disjointed as none of the services had co-operated operationally before except on internal counter-insurgency missions.

Elders in Argentine diplomacy were proud of their record as peacemakers. Argentina had been awarded the Nobel Prize for Peace in 1935 for finding a settlement to the Chaco War between Paraguay and Bolivia. Now the nation was going to war for the first time since the Paraguayan War of 1865, and was committed to having the invasion force ready by 15 September 1982, a date close to the British intention to scrap HMS *Endurance*. It was also by when Argentina's 14 new Dassault Super Étendard strike aircraft equipped with 16 AM39 air-launched Exocet missiles should be in service. An initial plan was for the covert occupation of South Georgia, however, Juan Lombardo insisted if the Falklands were the main objective, early occupation of South Georgia be cancelled. Galtieri and Anaya agreed but then, on 20 March, in Uruguay, Lombardo read in the press that Constantino Davidoff, a scrap merchant, had landed on South Georgia. Learning that he had been reinforced with a detachment of marines under Lieutenant Alfredo Astiz and furious at being double-crossed by his own service, he knew that Britain would react. The blue and white national flag raising by marines led to the passing of Resolution 502 at the UN, upholding British objections to the use of force and requiring Argentine withdrawal. Fearing a British response, on 25 March, Admiral Anaya gambled, ordering Carlos Büsser to ensure that the amphibious assets for Operation *Rosario* were ready to sail in 72 hours. Working intensely, Garcia Bol and Sigfrido Plessel brought Argentine air assets to operational status to support the invasion: Grumman S-2E Trackers, Lockheed P-2 Neptunes, Sikorsky S-61D-4 Sea Kings, Westland Lynx HAS23s, Fokker F-27s and F-28s, C-130 Hercules, de Havilland Canada DHC-3 Otters, Bell UH-1 Hueys, Hughes 500Cs, Boeing CH-47C Chinooks, Boeing 737s and Aérospatiale AS 332 Super Pumas. The war that would follow would be a rare example of a Cold War conflict in which both sides used western weaponry, with Argentina's equipment sourced largely from the United States, Britain, France, Germany and Israel.

Argentine troops landed on the Falkland Islands during the early hours of 2 April. LVTP-7 assault amphibious vehicles descended into the water from the landing ship ARA *Cabo Sa Antonio* (Q42) and were ashore by 0630hrs, one commanded by Lieutenant Colonel Mohamed Ali Seineldin of the *Regimiento de Infantería Mecanizado 25* (25th Mechanized Infantry Regiment), with three more LVTP-7s in support. Port Stanley airport was successfully taken, the runway littered with concrete blocks, and the odd vehicle in response to the invasion was cleared; then a Sea King from *2da Escuadrilla Aeronaval de Helicópteros* (2nd Naval Helicopter Squadron) touched down at 0734hrs. Within half an hour the first Grupo 1 fixed-wing Hercules C-130 transport from Comodoro Rivadavia landed. Air activity was high with continuous landings. Two C-130's stayed after offloading and obstructed half of the apron which slowed down the process

Four of the seven *Black Buck* missions used iron bombs; the remaining missions against Argentine mobile radar sites on the island used AGM-45A Shrike anti-radar missiles. The Vulcans were rapidly modified to carry two AGM-45A missiles on Skybolt wing pylons. (Crown Copyright MOD)

NORTH ATLANTIC
OCEAN

CAPE VERDE
ISLANDS

VENEZUELA

GUYANA

SURINAM

FRENCH
GUIANA

COLOMBIA

PERU

BRAZIL

BOLIVIA

PARAGUAY

Rio de Janeiro

San Felix

URUGUAY

CHILE

ARGENTINA

Ascension Island

Refuelling 1

Refuelling 3

Refuelling 1   Refuelling 2

Refuelling 3

Refuelling 2

SOUTH ATLANTIC
OCEAN

Refuelling 4

Trelew

Comodoro Rivadavia,
Air Force Southern Command

San Julián
Santa Cruz support base

Río Gallegos

FALKLAND ISLANDS

South Georgia

Río Grande

N

0   500 miles

0   500km

Argentinian air bases

Air bases used by RAF

Total Exclusion Zone (TEZ)

Black Buck flight route

Black Buck 6 diversion to Rio de Janeiro

Nimrod reconnaissance
off Argentina, 15 May

of unloading other transport aircraft and distributing equipment by VII Brigada Aérea's two Chinook helicopters. Major Brigadier Hellmuth Conrado Weber, Commander of Air Operations, also deployed Grupo 3's twenty-four FMA IA58 Pucará to Stanley with the support of the KC.130H Hercules TC-70. The first four arrived at 16.00hrs on 2 April to form the Pucará Malvinas Airmobile Squadron (*Malvinas Escuadrón Aeromóvil*), the first combat aircraft to land on the island. Guiding them down was the Air Surveillance and Control Group 1 (*Grupo de Vigilancia and Control Aéreo 1*).

The first casualty at Stanley airport was on 14 April, 1982. Rain and a strong wind whipped across the runway; the pilots of Fuerza Aérea Argentina (Argentine Air Force) Fokker F-28 TC-53 tried to touch down in the opposite direction but their excessive speed meant that the aircraft careered off the runway. Its left tyre burst and broke the nose gear. When it stopped, it was 50m from going into the sea, with tail raised at 45 degrees. Using M8A1 matting the runway was extended by 262ft to facilitate the removal of TC-53 coupled to a bulldozer. It was later repaired and transferred back to the mainland for continued service carrying military supplies and Exocet missiles.

It was therefore imperative that the focus of the Argentinian Army was the tactical air defence of the only significant airport in the Malvinas from low-altitude attack. The Argentine defence system was formidable, combining the best features of British and European systems; if permitted to function as designed, the air defence array was capable of effective protection to key targets on the Malvinas. Recognition of this, and of the versatility of the Argentinian radar systems, surface-to-air missiles, and the possibility of Exocet missiles being deployed to the islands drove Admiral Sandy Woodward, and planners at Northwood as they strove to craft plans to dismantle this capability.

Air defence

Prior to Operation *Rosario,* Argentine Army units for air defence comprised *Grupo de Aérea Defensa 601* and *Grupo de Aérea Defensa 602* (GADA 601 and GADA 602, 601st and 602nd Air Defence Groups). Each was mobilized on 12 April, then deployed to East Falkland (Soledad Island). There they formed the nucleus of *1° Grupo de Defensa* (1st Defence Group) AAA. Commanded by Major Hugo Maiorano, this group was deployed to garrison the airfields on the islands. It was made up of 3rd Batería with 35mm Oerlikon GDF-002 35/90 guns, under the command of First Lieutenant Oscar Spath, and 4th Batería under the command of First Lieutenant Félix Dalves with nine Rheinmetall RH 202 20mm guns, and 15,000 rounds. Since arriving on 2 April, 4th Batería were stationed at Stanley airfield (*Puerto Argentino*) with Dalves installing their AN/TPS43 radar in the airport area, near the coast. On April 12, there was a change of location for Dalves to the outskirts of Stanley, to become better camouflaged. 820ft from their radar, located in Government House, was the Command and Control Centre for the entire air defence of the islands, together with the anti-aircraft defence command post nearby. Integral to that defence was AN/TPS-43 and AN/TPS-43F exploration radar with a maximum range radius of 425km (264 miles), and a Swiss-made Super Fledermaus which provided fire control for the three 35mm Oerlikon GDF-002 35/90 pieces, and gave a 4km (2.5-mile) umbrella of defence with a 360-degree coverage. It also had nine 20mm RH 202 twin cannons for close defence. A TPS-43 radar was used to locate enemy threats, for air traffic control, and for directing fighters against British forces. The system furnished coverage from low altitude through mid-stratosphere and its operators were attached from *Grupo 2 Vigilancia Aérea y Control de Tráfico Aéreo Militar* (Group 2 of Air Surveillance and Military Air Traffic Control). It was linked to the centre in Government House to establish engagement priorities. At Goose Green Maiorano deployed the 7th Batería, with an Israeli ELTA portable scanning radar (purchased in 1980) for target indication with a 20km (12.4 mile) range with six Rheinmetall RH 202 20mm twin cannons.

The naval element *Infanteria de Marina* (Marine Infantry) had shared responsibility for air defence and was integrated with Maiorano's 1º Grupo de Defensa AAA to coordinate Stanley's AAA, effectively combining to defend against enemy aircraft or helicopters. Infanteria de Marina came under the command of Marine Major Hector Silva. They deployed to the Falkland Islands with three triple SAM Tigercat launchers (with their trio portable optronics and radio guidance directions) and 12 single-barrel 30mm Hispano Suiza HS-831 cannons. The battalion was deployed in three sectors covering 360-degrees of the airfield. Each sector had three 30mm cannons and a triple Tigercat launcher.

As of 2 April 1982, the British did not know the operational strength or capabilities of the Argentine Air Defence on the Falkland Islands. However, Argentina had deployed 15 Oerlikon GDF-002 25/90s; one Contraves Super Fledermaus fire-control system; six units of Contraves Skyguard fire-control systems (the Super Fledermaus' replacement); 15 20mm Rheinmetall RH 202 twin-barrel cannons; one Roland SAM post; seven triple Tigercat SAM posts; 20 30mm Hispano-Suiza HS-831 cannons; three Oerlikon 20/120 20mm cannons; one Westinghouse AN/TPS-43 radar (3D); one Cardion TPS-44 radar (2D) and two ELTA portable radars; plus the numerous handheld Blowpipes (60 initially) and SA-7 Strela (170 initially) that were available to Argentine troops.

Most AAA systems were initially clustered around a defensive point – Port Stanley airfield. Lieutenant Colonel Héctor Lubin Arias of GADA 601 was then tasked to deploy a Cardion TPS-44 Mk II and Contraves Skyguard with 12 Oerlikon 35mm GDF-002 35/90s to Sapper Hill (*Cerro Zapador*) and Goose Green (*Goose Prairie*); while Second Lieutenant Claudio Oscar Braghini of 3a Section Batería B /101 deployed two Oerlikon 35/90 GDF-002 cannons, with two generator sets, one Skyguard and 280 boxes of 35mm ammunition to Goose Green.

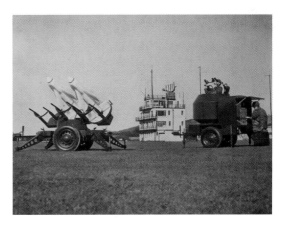

Tigercat trailer-mounted launcher with an operator seated at the fire-control equipment in the early 1970s in Britain for a demonstration. This short-range surface-to-air missile (SAM) system equipped the GADA Mix 602 missile battery jointly with the Franco-German Roland SAM system which began to arrive in early 1982. A total of seven Tigercat missile launchers were deployed; there were several near misses, but no confirmed losses. (Andrew D. Bird Collection)

Argentine air defence units on the Malvinas
Grupo de Aerea Defensa 601 | Commanded by Lieutenant Colonel Héctor Arias
Cardion AN/TPS-44 Alert Mk II A/O scanning radar, with maximum range of about 400km (250 miles)
Oerlikon Skyguard Rheinmetall Defense system integrating the Skyguard fire-control system, used to control 12 Oerlikon Contraves twin 35mm GDF-002 35/90 series towed anti-aircraft guns
A complement of 429 men: 26 officers, 117 non-commissioned officers and 286 soldiers – operators or technicians
Total number of support vehicles deployed from the mainland was 13: one jeep, five Dodge-type light trucks and seven trucks. GADA 601 had the most motorized vehicles in the entire deployment to Malvinas, so supported the other units.
Grupo de Aerea Defensa 602 | Overall command of First Lieutenant Carlos Leónidas Regalini
Towed SAM Roland missile launcher (all-weather version with radar and/or optronic guidance), commanded by Second Lieutenant Diego Noguer.
Three Oerlikon 20mm anti-aircraft guns, with ammunition stocks comprising 16,000 rounds of 20mm cannon shells, commanded by Second Lieutenant Rodolfo Sánchez with 20 men (operators or technicians)
Four triple SAM Tigercat missile launchers, with four Dodge-type light trucks, two tow launchers, with second trailer with fire-control equipment
The staff of 602 unit were included in the GADA 601 nominal roll

OPPOSITE RAF AIRFIELDS IN *BLACK BUCK*

Batería B Grupo de Artillería AAA 101 (GADA 101) | Commanded by Major Jorge Alberto Monge
Eight single-barrel 30mm Hispano Suiza HS-831 cannons
Ten Browning machine guns 12.7mm, ammunition stocks comprising 16,000 rounds
101 GADA deployed to the islands with three officers, 19 non-commissioned officers and 90 soldiers: total 112 men
One jeep, one Dodge-type light truck and five trucks
El Batallón a.a. de La Infantería de Marina | Commanded by Marine Major Hector Silva
Estimated complement of 20 men – operators or technicians
Three triple SAM Tigercat missile launchers, with three Dodge-type light trucks, two tow launchers, with second trailer with fire-control equipment
12 single-barrel 30mm Hispano Suiza HS-831 cannons
Complement of 250 men including officers, non-commissioned officers and marine gunners or technicians/operators.

The move to the Malvinas

During the mid-1970s, GADA 601 had confronted the People's Revolutionary Army (ERP) guerrillas, led by 39-year-old Mario Roberto Santucho. A *coup d'état* in March 1976 saw the military Junta overthrow all constitutional, national and provincial authorities, deposing the country's president, Maria Estela Martinez. GADA 601 was based at the headquarters of Subzone 15 from where illegal methods of torture, murder and disappearances were carried out during the so-called Dirty War.

Two years later, on 12 December 1978, GADA 601 moved to north-western Patagonia with GADA 602 in the build-up of military forces during the Beagle Channel dispute with Chile, establishing AAA sites at Black River, Colorado River and Limay River to defend key bridges. January 1979 saw them quartered in Patagonia. During those four years GADA 601

One of the Argentine Skyguard cabins blending in with its surroundings on the Falkland Islands. (Andrew D. Bird Collection)

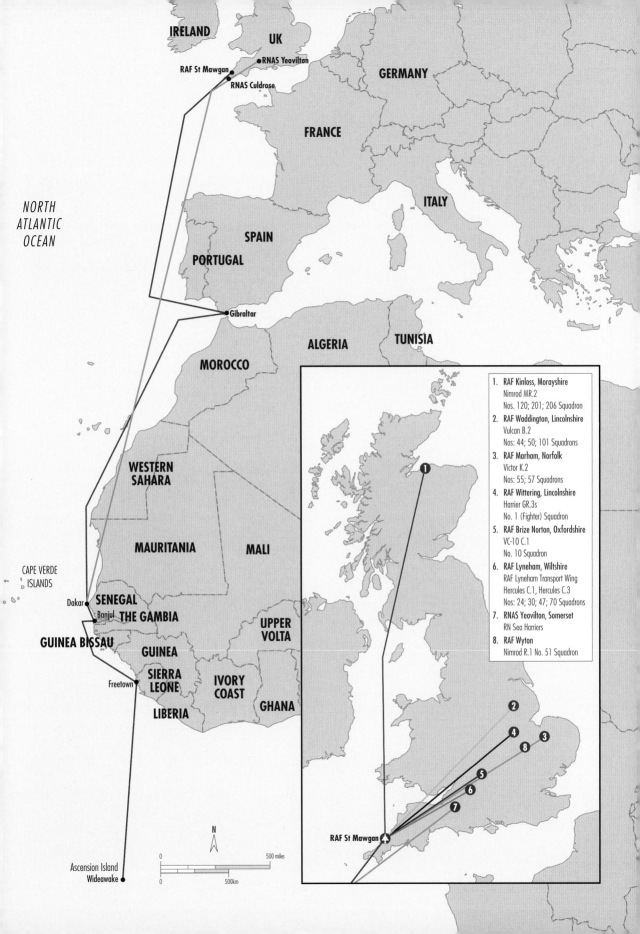

NORTH
ATLANTIC
OCEAN

IRELAND

UK

GERMANY

RNAS Yeovilton
RAF St Mawgan
RNAS Culdrose

FRANCE

ITALY

SPAIN

PORTUGAL

Gibraltar

ALGERIA

TUNISIA

MOROCCO

WESTERN
SAHARA

CAPE VERDE
ISLANDS

MAURITANIA

MALI

Dakar
SENEGAL
Banjul
THE GAMBIA

UPPER
VOLTA

GUINEA BISSAU

GUINEA

SIERRA
LEONE
Freetown

IVORY
COAST

GHANA

LIBERIA

Ascension Island
Wideawake

N

0   500 miles
0   500km

1. RAF Kinloss, Morayshire
   Nimrod MR.2
   Nos. 120; 201; 206 Squadron

2. RAF Waddington, Lincolnshire
   Vulcan B.2
   Nos: 44; 50; 101 Squadrons

3. RAF Marham, Norfolk
   Victor K.2
   Nos: 55; 57 Squadrons

4. RAF Wittering, Lincolnshire
   Harrier GR.3s
   No. 1 (Fighter) Squadron

5. RAF Brize Norton, Oxfordshire
   VC-10 C.1
   No. 10 Squadron

6. RAF Lyneham, Wiltshire
   RAF Lyneham Transport Wing
   Hercules C.1, Hercules C.3
   Nos: 24; 30; 47; 70 Squadrons

7. RNAS Yeovilton, Somerset
   RN Sea Harriers

8. RAF Wyton
   Nimrod R.1 No. 51 Squadron

RAF St Mawgan

and GADA 602 had received new military hardware, and their men received initial training in various European countries, becoming technically proficient on weapons and radar; they then enhanced these skills on programmes and exercises in the United States and South America, which further honed their readiness.

Nine days after General Leopoldo Galtieri launched Argentina's invasion on 11 April, at the end of Holy Week, GADA 601's commander Lieutenant Colonel Coronel Héctor Arias was informed that his unit would leave the next day for the Malvinas. Men returning home to their parents, wives or families from a Sunday out found that the police were waiting for them at the door.

It was a logistical nightmare at Mar del Plata, so weapons, ammunition, men and vehicles were airlifted to Comodoro Rivadavia. GADA 602 was then suddenly tasked by Buenos Aires with homeland air defence, deploying one Roland missile system with Skyguard radar and two Oerlikon 35mm twin cannons at two international airports: Puerto San Julián base for Dagger fighters, and Rio Gallegos which had Mirage III, and A-4 Skyhawks. Air defence was provided at other city airports housing Argentine naval and air force jets. Arias and 2nd Lieutenant Diego Noguer, commander of GADA 602, with a group of men from both units then flew by Hercules and arrived on the islands between 12 April and 24 April, and were given defensive positions near the airport. On 17 April Hercules C-130 CT-64 landed at Stanley airport (BAM Malvinas). GADA 601's 35mm AAA and Skyguard was offloaded. Arias met a Spanish civilian technician from the Oerlikon company, Eusebio Aguiar, who checked the cannons and Skyguard fire-control system for optimization before being deployed.

The ship *Río Carcarañá*, berthed in Buenos Aires, was being loaded with equipment and supplies for Batería B Grupo de Artillería AAA 101 (B/GADA 101): eight Hispano Suiza 30mm cannons and heavy vehicles with crates containing munitions and other logistics, with corporals Rubén Reynaldo Pardini and Raúl Orlando Barrios in charge of loading. The merchant ship, with its civilian crew, sailed on 22 April for Port Stanley, dropping anchor outside the harbour. The cargo ship *Formosa* was already berthed and unloading heavy machinery. Hours passed before Lieutenant Primero Alejandro Infantino of 101 B/GADA offloaded enough from *Río Carcarañá* to get his section underway before the merchant ship was shuffled back outside the harbour. The tanker *Río Cincel* then offloaded pallets containing 800 drums of JP-1 jet fuel assigned to Stanley airport.[1]

Earlier, on 5 April, the *Grupo 1 de Construcciones* (Runway Construction Unit) led by Major Raúl Oscar Maiorano arrived, accompanied by Senior Petty Officer Gerardo González, Assistant Petty Officer Ricardo Diax, Petty Officers Alberto Natalino and Miguel Muñoz. Corporals Erio Moyano, Edgardo Acosta, Victor Gutiérrez and Carlos Monyoya arrived by Hercules C-130. In order for all Argentine aircraft to be able to operate from Port Stanley, it was essential to expand the runway at Stanley airport. Machinery was shipped by Empresa Líneas Marítimas Argentinas (ELMA) *Formosa*, a 12,762-ton cargo ship. It transported 200 M8A1 metal mats, along with tools, equipment and machines to facilitate an extension. At the airfield, Maiorano received orders to construct fortifications and participate in the unloading of *Rio Cincel,* then utilize dump trucks to transport troops. At the time, BAM Malvinas commander Commodore Héctor Luis Destri didn't understand the importance of extending the runway to increase the operational capacity of the base. The threat of British submarines, and exclusion zones neutralized ELMA seaborne supply lines. Weber, Commander of Air Operations in Argentina, now had to build an airbridge in order for these aircraft to operate. It was essential to expand the small airfield.

---

1   Tanker *Río Cincel* was at anchor on 1 May, and strafed by Sea Harriers' 30mm cannons. Ship's captain Edgardo Dell'Ellicine then sailed the tanker to San Carlos, East Falklands.

Grupo 1 de Construccione:mechanical machinery/equipment	Quantity
Caterpillar D-7 bulldozer	2
Astarsa motor grader 120/120 AWD	1
Caterpillar 995-12 front loader	1
Caterpillar 977 track loader	1
Mercedes-Benz 1,114 dump trucks	2
Mercedes-Benz Unimog flatbed truck	1
Koeating 285 KVA generator	2
Jeep	1
M8A1 landing mat (with various fix attachments) 22in by 144in (560mm x 3,660mm)	200
Tar bitumen blocks	75

At a quarry 12.5 miles from Stanley, Grupo I de Construcciones had their two D-7 bulldozers, a 977 track loader, and four dump trucks, which went to work extracting gravel for foundations for airport extensions. Due to the lack of roads, these machines had to be airlifted to the quarry suspended from cargo hooks of Chinook helicopters. The building project would increase airport capacity by 38,750 sq ft near the control tower. Other areas were repaired or fully replaced using aluminium planking.

With hostilities imminent it was necessary for Raúl Oscar Maiorano's men to be on immediate readiness to repair the runway in the event that it was hit by bombing or naval gunfire. The unit's numbers were increased in the early hours on 13 April, when an F-28 brought reinforcements. Off stepped Lieutenant Ignacio Galardi, with Corporal Euardo Cubi to work as machinist on the Astarsa, along with two civilians, Carlos Alfonso Corona and Carlos Albert Corona. All then began other non-specific tasks, including transporting medical staff and medical supplies into Stanley to a building considered to be the safest for a surgical centre. Lack of coordination following the loss of the ARA *General Belgrano* on 2 May and the previous days first *Black Buck* and Sea Harrier raids, meant the idea of extending the Stanley airport runway to accommodate a fleet of transports and their fighter jets stalled. Further quantities of M8A1 aluminium planking and tar bitumen blocks were on board an ELMA cargo ship that could not now sail, due to the dangers of submarine attack.

Aftermath of *Black Buck 1* on 1 May 1982. Aerial reconnaissance photograph taken using a Vinten F.95 camera flown by Lieutenant Commander Neill Thomas, commander of No. 899 Naval Air Squadron, Fleet Air Arm aboard HMS *Hermes*. (Crown Copyright MOD)

CAMPAIGN OBJECTIVES
The expedition takes shape

The service chiefs at a conference at Fleet Headquarters, Northwood. They include Field Marshal Edwin Bramall in the immediate foreground on the right; Admiral of the Fleet Sir Henry Conyers Leach and Air Chief- Marshal Sir Michael James Beetham on the left, second and third in. (Andrew D. Bird Collection)

The British resolution adopted by the Security Council as Resolution 502 on April 3 demanded the 'immediate cessation of hostilities' and the 'immediate withdrawal of all Argentine forces' from the Falkland Islands *(Islas Malvinas)* and called upon the Argentine and British Governments to 'seek a diplomatic solution to their differences.' Resolution 502 was in Britain's favour, giving it the option to invoke Article 51 of the UN Charter and claim the right of self-defence. It was supported by members of the Commonwealth and by the European Union, which later imposed sanctions on Argentina. In Washington, British Ambassador Nicholas 'Nicko' Henderson was asked if his government had considered getting the Vatican involved in trying to resolve the dispute. In his opinion the Argentines would not listen to the Vatican, if they wouldn't listen to the President of the United States. On Prime Minister Margaret Thatcher's orders, a few days earlier the Royal Fleet Auxiliary *Fort Austin* in the Mediterranean steamed to support HMS *Endurance*, with two nuclear-powered submarines HMS *Spartan* (from Gibraltar) and HMS *Splendid* (from Scotland). On 31 March, serious doubts were raised during a meeting in the House of Commons, in Margaret Thatcher's office, by Defence Secretary John Nott and other senior government advisers arguing that retaking the island was an impossibility because of logistical difficulties. However, the 'knight in shining gold braid', First Sea Lord Sir Henry Leach, who joined this critical discussion advised that the Falklands not only could be recaptured, but should be. The ships would take three weeks to reach the South Atlantic, and the two small carriers, HMS *Hermes* and HMS *Invincible*, could provide sufficient air cover. This was greeted by the Prime Minister with relief and approval, for had Chief of the Defence Staff Lord Lewin been present, he would probably have counselled caution and emphasized diplomacy.

In the early hours of 2 April *Hermes* and *Invincible* were put on four hours' alert, as was *Fearless*, the amphibious assault ship, the frigates *Alacrity* and *Antelope* and the RFA *Resource*. At 0300hrs, Admiral Sandy Woodward received the signal from the commander-in-chief ordering Operation *Corporate*, the codename for everything that was to follow.

Over the weekend a task force was prepared, with pandemonium breaking out at naval bases as 100 ships were pulled together and some 50 civilian ships requisitioned for supplies. Leach was terrified that the Cabinet would get cold feet and rescind the task force.

On 3 April Margaret Thatcher spoke in the House of Commons: 'The House meets this Saturday to respond to a situation of great gravity,' said the Prime Minister, 'We are here because, for the first

Vulcan XM598 on the apron, with Pan Am pick-ups in the foreground. (Crown Copyright MOD)

time for many years, British sovereign territory has been invaded by a foreign power.' The vanguard of the largest British fleet deployed since World War II sailed from Portsmouth harbour to rapturous applause on the Monday morning. Francis Pym, the leader of the House of Commons, was chosen to take over immediately at the Foreign Office. The small War Cabinet consisted of Willie Whitelaw, the Home Secretary; John Nott, the Defence Secretary; Francis Pym, the Foreign Secretary, and Cecil Parkinson, the Trade and Industry secretary. Air Chief-Marshal Sir Michael Beetham, the Chief of the Air Staff and acting Chief of the Defence Staff (for Chief of the Defence Staff Admiral Terence Lewin was in New Zealand), arrived to give a military briefing with a bleary-eyed Admiral Leach, who like Beetham had worked through the night with only a 30-minute nap. Although Margaret Thatcher had emphatically called for 'the nation to stand and fight', there were concerns over casualties, if war really came.

The defence chiefs, led by Lewin, had routinely reviewed the Falkland Islands, and held the consensus that they were indefensible in modern warfare, given that the nearest airfield and anchorage was Ascension Island. Therefore no well-formed national war plans stood to meet such a contingency. That doctrine was abandoned once the Argentines occupied the islands. Leach turned to Admiral Sir John Fieldhouse, Commander-in-Chief of Fleet at the Northwood headquarters, appointing him commander of Task Force 317 and giving him responsibility for Operation *Corporate* with the mission to recover the Falkland Islands. Co-located with Commander-in-Chief of Fleet was Air Marshal Sir John Curtiss, Air Officer Commanding No. 18 Group, where he commanded the RAF's maritime air assets. The two men had a strong rapport and Curtiss became Fieldhouse's air commander, an obvious appointment since his command specialized in maritime air power and his staff were accustomed to working well alongside the Royal Navy.

Curtiss became part of Flag and Air Officers (FLAIR) with Admiral Sir Peter Herbert, the Royal Navy's Flag Officer Submarines; Admiral David Hallifax, the chief of staff to Fieldhouse, responsible for the day-to-day control of Northwood; Admiral Peter Hammersley, Chief Staff Officer Engineering; General Jeremy Moore, Royal Marines; then a late addition, Lieutenant General Richard Trant, who succeeded Moore as an adviser when he flew south to become overall commander of British land forces for the invasion of the Falkland Islands. Moore realized that the British Army also faced limitations on what forces could be committed. Although there was no general mobilization, army units were recalled. Of the 160,000 soldiers in the regular army in 1982, 55,000 were in West Germany, with other garrisons based in Berlin, Hong Kong, Gibraltar, Belize, Brunei and Cyprus. There were also around 11,000 troops serving in Northern Ireland.

The first of Fieldhouse's calls to Beetham was to establish an air bridge to Ascension, and reconnaissance flights ahead of the Task Force during its voyage south. With overseas bases

OPPOSITE AIR DEFENCE AT PORT STANLEY

along the route having long since disappeared, Francis Pym enquired about using Sierra Leone's facilities. A formal request to support five British aircraft flying into the US military air base on Ascension over a four-day period was sent by the Ministry of Defence to the Pentagon. The two Pan Am air traffic controllers guided down the first five C-130 Hercules from Brize Norton and Lyneham, each with an estimated 45,000lb load. A series of further Hercules and VC-10 flights established the base as the forward logistic support for British forces on Operation *Corporate*.

Nimrod MR.1s operating from St Mawgan and Gibraltar carried out surveillance over the waters through which the various elements of the Task Groups were transiting. With such prodigious distances involved, the need for in-flight refuelling became paramount for extending the range of air assets. John Curtiss quickly received funds to update all the Victor K.2 tanker force with the latest navigation equipment. However, their first priority was reconnaissance, and it was necessary to tackle the problems that the Nimrod fleet did not possess an air-to-air refuelling capability and that No. 27 Squadron, which had been assigned the task of maritime radar reconnaissance (MRR) with its Vulcan B.2s, had disbanded on 31 March.

Curtiss conveyed his concerns, and quickly asked for five of the navigation radar operators from the Vulcan B.2 (MRRs) to be retained. Victor K.2s XL192, XL164 and XL189 were converted to fly photo-reconnaissance and MRR with an upgraded navigation system for long-range flights over water from Ascension, which could acquire intelligence on Argentine naval forces for the Royal Navy. While preparations were made for their deployment, John Fieldhouse asked Curtiss for them to seek out the Argentinians' six ships in the region of South Georgia, including the aircraft carrier ARA *Veinticinco de Mayo* and cruiser *General Belgrano*. Intelligence then revealed that nearly every Argentinian warship was equipped with Exocet missiles. If any got within range the loss of one carrier would have impeded the British operation. 'Could their aircraft carrier launch the Super Étendard?' enquired Assistant Chief of the Air Staff (Operations) Air Vice-Marshal Ken Hayr, worried about the air threat to the Task Force.

Nose of a Vulcan viewed through the cockpit while ahead are contrails from a Victor tanker. (Crown Copyright MOD)

With the Task Force getting ever nearer, the Argentines had to be prevented from deploying, or persuaded not to deploy, their high-performance Skyhawks, Mirages and Super Étendards into Port Stanley airport. However, Fieldhouse and Curtiss had overlooked the potential of their Grumman S-2E Trackers, not just in their anti-submarine warfare role but also as reconnaissance aircraft, with an ability to fly 1,173nm (1,350 miles) and an endurance of nearly nine hours. These aircraft were operated from *Veinticinco de Mayo*, off the Argentinian mainland, or from Stanley airport from where they could easily detect the Task Force. Unknown to Northwood, since 3 April two S-2Es had been permanently based on the island

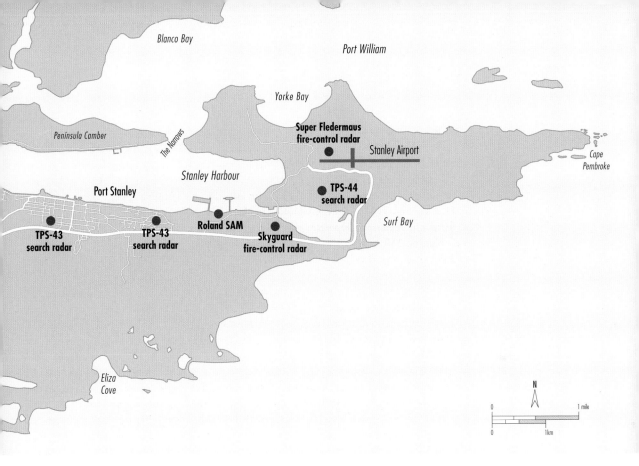

Blanco Bay

Port William

Yorke Bay

Super Fledermaus
fire-control radar

Stanley Airport

Península Camber

The Narrows

Cape
Pembroke

TPS-44
search radar

Stanley Harbour

Port Stanley

Surf Bay

Roland SAM

TPS-43
search radar

TPS-43
search radar

Skyguard
fire-control radar

Eliza
Cove

N

0   1 mile

0   1km

and begun anti-submarine warfare patrols over their shipping lanes, while three were deployed on the aircraft carrier.[2]

Sea Harriers or Vulcans?

On 11 April Sandy Woodward requested plans for how best to utilize Sea Harriers to attack targets on the Falklands. This nudged Beetham into examining if and how to use the only RAF bomber aircraft capable of carrying a conventional payload – the Vulcan. One of the first issues planning staff had to work out was the feasibility of air attacks against Argentine cities or ports, launched from Ascension Island. With limited numbers of Victor tankers and because of the distance involved in the approach, the aircraft would have to land in South America after an attack, possibly in Montevideo or Santiago in Uruguay. Britain's ambassador to Uruguay, Patricia Hutchinson, believed that a request would be denied, for Argentina was already putting pressure on Uruguay, insisting that no British military aircraft be allowed to land in the country's airports or military bases. Planning staff agreed that bombing or torpedo attacks could, however, be carried out on Argentine shipping in the South Atlantic within range of Ascension. It was contested as to whether bombing the mainland would be legal, but in the long term it would be undesirable, losing Britain influence, allies and trade. However, both Britain and Argentina could calculate that mainland targets could be struck from Ascension. As soon as it was realized that Vulcans had been deployed to Wideawake, this implication added pressure to Galtieri and his Junta. There was speculation as to whether

2   During the war Escuadrilla Aeronaval Antisubmarina EA2S S-2E Trackers carried out 112 missions, completing more than 520 flying hours without any casualties.

Avro Vulcan XM607 landing at Greenham Common, Berkshire for the annual International Air Show in June 1977. (Andrew D. Bird Collection)

this was merely public posturing, or a valid military option. Press speculation that the RAF's Vulcan force might be used to attack Argentina was not actively discouraged.

Analysis of the airfield

Of the airfields available on the Falklands, it was quickly concluded by Wing Commander Simon Baldwin's planning team that only Port Stanley airport with its paved runway was capable of sustaining major operations; Goose Green and Pebble Island were discounted. Stanley facilities, although limited, were able to accommodate C-130 Hercules, Lockheed L-188 Electra and Fokker F-27 and F28 transports; also Boeing 737 commercial jets to bring supplies, weapons, vehicles, and fuel, for an expanding Argentine garrison.

Port Stanley's length of runway was a comparative size to Popham grass strip near Basingstoke in Hampshire, and some Argentinian aircraft were capable of operating from the existing runway. The Italian-manufactured Aermacchi MB-339 advanced trainer had a supplementary close-air support role, as did the American propeller-driven Beech T-34 Turbo-Mentor and the FMA Pucarás. These could all prove a threat to the amphibious phase when reclaiming the Falklands.

Nevertheless, Stanley was assessed as unsuitable for basing the most capable and advanced jets, such as the Mirage III, A-4 Skyhawk, Dagger and Super Étendard, given the relatively short runway. There was naivety in this initial assessment, however, as it was assumed that the Argentines would not make any attempts to extend the runway or the parking aprons. In fact, this would be given serious consideration by the Argentinian Air Force, as jets based at Stanley could attack the British Task Force as it approached the islands. A senior officer from one of the Royal Engineers' field squadrons supporting the RAF's Harriers in Germany gave an assessment: with some forward planning and work by Argentine engineers, it would be entirely possible to base at least four to six fast jet aircraft at Stanley, giving a limited fighter defence capability to the islands. The only limiting factor was the availability of fuel storage for the aircraft. But no doubt Pillow portable fuel tanks that hold 95,000 litres would be ferried in.

Defence Secretary John Nott raised concerns that it would provide the Argentines with a publicity coup were they to reveal that work had been undertaken to allow fast jet operations from Stanley. US intelligence reported that Argentina was lengthening the runway at Stanley by 2,000m in order to accommodate transport and combat aircraft. It was clear that the runway at Port Stanley would pose a considerable threat to Woodward's task force, particularly when the carriers were in the vicinity of the Falklands. Fieldhouse and Curtiss, in consultation with the Task Force commander, agreed that for Admiral Woodward to maintain control of the sea and air, it would be vital to deny Argentinian jets the use of Port Stanley, in conjunction with the Exclusion Zone around the islands.

The beginning of the air war

However, Woodward was soon within range of Argentina's mainland-based long-range search aircraft. On 21 April, *Hermes* radar operators registered a high-altitude unidentified air contact. Lieutenant Simon Hargreaves on QRF (Quick Reaction Force duty) in Sea Harrier XZ460 was scrambled to intercept. His quarry, Boeing 707-387C TC-91, had taken off from El Palomar at 0458hrs, on its first mission of the campaign. Using its Bendix weather radar on mapping mode, with a range of 240nm, the crew began searching for the British Task Force. Visual contact was confirmed at 1238hrs when a 707 crew saw the aircraft carriers HMS *Hermes* and HMS *Invincible*, with destroyers and frigates, from 20,000ft. Captain Luis Dupeyron of the Argentine Navy recognized both carriers and immediately ordered the pilots to rapidly leave the area and climb, noticing that the carriers were facing into the wind ready for aircraft to launch. At 1247hrs they commenced the climb, then three minutes later, a technician observed an aircraft streaking towards them. Hargreaves positioned his Sea Harrier armed with two Sidewinders beneath its wings on the portside and inspected the 707-387C TC-91. The pursuit above 30,000ft lasted for 12 minutes, after which Hargreaves returned to *Hermes*. This was the first information that Argentina had obtained for themselves about the approaching Task Force. Regular encounters began between Sea Harriers and Boeing TC-91 and TC-92, of Escuadrón V-I Brigada Aérea.

The Task Force was no longer out of reach. Its use of Sea Harriers in disrupting Argentine operations out of Port Stanley was brought to the table at Northwood. Both military Chiefs of Staff wanted to preserve the Task Force's small and outnumbered Sea Harrier force for the vital priority of air defence, confirmed in the concept of air operations agreed on 28 April. Then Woodward was told on 29 April that the Vulcan bombing run was planned for 1 May at 0700hrs: Chiefs of Staff had agreed that the Vulcan had the advantage over the Sea Harrier in its blind bombing capability if the weather should close in. Fieldhouse also eased one of Brigadier Julian Thompson's, commander of 3 Commando Brigade, preoccupations by declaring firmly that any landing on the Falkland Islands would not take place under an Argentine air threat: that meant neutralizing Stanley airport first.

AGM-45 Shrike missiles on the port wing hardpoint of Vulcan XM597 at Waddington. The photo was taken after 13 June 1982, as the nose shows two Shrike mission symbols and the Brazilian flag for its stay in Brazil. (Crown Copyright MOD)

THE CAMPAIGN
The RAF's last heavy bomber campaign

Avro Vulcan XM598 arriving at Ascension Island's Wideawake airfield on 29 April, taxiing onto the apron with Green Mountain in the background. (Crown Copyright, MOD)

The US government came down on the side of the British on 30 April. In Buenos Aires, Galtieri was baffled as Washington imposed military and economic sanctions on Argentina. He had seen the Reagan administration as his friend. Economic sanctions were widely criticized in Latin America for the act of siding with a power outside the hemisphere. Brazil's President João Figueiredo, the last president from the period of the military dictatorship, met with President Reagan and requested that a solution to the crisis be found. But Brazil's military regime's 'neutrality' stance was paper-thin as Galtieri took the opportunity to secure arms from around the globe. The first contact from Soviet diplomats offering support to Argentina occurred a week after the conflict began, on 9 April, according to the Brazilian Navy. A Cuban aircraft carrying munitions for Argentina made an unauthorized entrance into Brazilian airspace causing an incident since, at the time, Brazil and Havana had cut off diplomatic relations. The situation was resolved following six hours of discussions with Argentine diplomats, and the aircraft was allowed to continue. The Brazilian Ministry of Foreign Affairs then recommended 'favourable treatment' to requests from Argentina, including trade operations to purchase weapons. These were clandestinely smuggled through Brazil using the airports of Recife (Pernambuco, north-east Brazil) and Río de Janeiro for an air bridge.

After weeks and thousands of air miles on shuttle diplomacy, Secretary of State Alexander Haig tried to convey to João Figueiredo that the Argentinian military Junta had made a serious miscalculation in thinking that a powerful Western democracy was too soft, too decadent to defend itself, and that Argentina was now the greatest danger to peace in South America. 'British victory is far from guaranteed as military action is full of risks,' commented Figueiredo.

With the final restraint on the British military action removed, tensions increased amongst Argentinian forces on the Falklands as they waited for a full-frontal assault. The Task Force was about 250 miles westwards, outside the Maritime Exclusion Zone (MEZ), when new rules of engagement came from London. When inside the MEZ Admiral Sandy Woodward had permission to open fire on any military ship or aircraft identified as Argentinian. Fieldhouse, on a satellite link from Northwood, informed Admiral Woodward that missions were to be intensified in order to start the process of recapturing the Falkland Islands. Critical information about the Argentinian naval groups led to the discovery, up to the north-west, of the aircraft carrier *Veinticinco de Mayo*, with its two escorting destroyers. On its deck were A-4 Skyhawks and Super Étendards. Down to the south-west was the heavily armed cruiser *General Belgrano* (formally USS *Phoenix*) with Type 42 destroyer escorts, each carrying eight Exocet missiles. Fieldhouse's central concern was the aircraft carrier; it was preferable that this threat be removed from the Argentinian Order of Battle.

Final countdown: *Black Buck 1*

On Tuesday 27 April, Squadron Leader Mel James, in charge of the Vulcan engineering detachment, departed Waddington for RAF Brize Norton at 1500hrs with five technicians, using an HS 780 Andover CC.2 of the RAF's Queen's Flight. They departed by VC-10 at 1800hrs for Ascension, routed via Banjul, Gambia and Dakar in Senegal. Squadron Leader Alastair Montgomery was nominated as detachment commander, and his crew were also on board, as the operations crew.

Two C-130Ks with the remaining 25 technicians departed at 2230hrs and 0330hrs. Air France staff at Dakar provided sandwiches and liquid refreshments to sustain the airmen to Ascension. At Waddington each member of the Vulcan crews was issued with a Browning 9mm automatic pistol and prepared for the nine-hour flight to Ascension. XM598 and XM607 after two in-flight refuellings arrived at 1800hrs on 29 April; an enquiry on their combat readiness found XM598 ready, while XM607 required maintenance.

In Northwood, London, John Fieldhouse was authorized by the government to launch the raid on Stanley airport. But before preparations began, *Black Buck 1* was compromised. Discussions in Washington on UN proposals that the British might accept, provided full-scale fighting had not yet begun, saw Haig reveal to Foreign Minister Costa Mendez 'according to our information a British attack could begin as early as Friday, 30 April.'[3] However, word had already reached Stanley airport.

Preparations began at 0850hrs on Ascension's Wideawake air base, when Group Captain Jerry Price received the Air Tasking message for Operation *Black Buck*, the codename given for the mission. This message added further detail to the Operations Order the previous day, but not the signal to execute the order for *Black Buck 1*. Price and other officers had to make sure there was nothing to prevent the Vulcans, Victors and Nimrods from carrying out their orders. The last aircraft to touch down before the mission were two Victors from Marham. Both turned off the single runway for the crowded flight line, where William Bryden's team marshalled them into vacant lots with millimetres to spare. There were now 14 Victors at Wideawake – half of the RAF's complete air-to-air refuelling fleet.

In their '5557 MASH Air Battle Fleet' marquee, the Victor operations team of

014 XM607 in flight showing a Shrike anti-radar AGM-45 on the port side, with AN/ALQ-10D ECM Dash-10 pod on the starboard side, used to counter radar-guided weapons. (Crown Copyright MOD)

3   Reagan Library, Executive Secretariat, NSC Cable File, Falkland File 04/28/1982.

Bob Tuxford's crew
standing by the entrance
to their operations tent
with the board of '5557
MASH Air Battle Fleet' in
homage to Hawkeye et al
from the MASH tv series.
Left to right: captain Bob
Tuxford; navigator radar
Ernie Wallis; co-pilot Glyn
Rees; air electronics officer
Mick Beer; and navigator
plotter John Keeble after
Black Buck's success.
(Brian Armstrong)

Trevor Sitch, Barry Ireland, David Davenall and Colin Haigh recalculated the previous day's draft of their refuelling plan with Jerry Price. Applying procedures developed over many years, and more recently enhanced by their maritime radar reconnaissance (MRR) excursion to South Georgia looking for any signs of the Argentine Navy, they worked out how fuel was to be swapped between the aircraft using ballpoint pens, pencils, slide rules, paper and performance tables, with a single digital pocket calculator. The outbound formation would consist of 11 Victor K.2s, each part of White, Red, or Blue Section, including two reserve aircraft; they were assigned to the primary Vulcan of Squadron Leader John Reeve and airborne reserve Flight Lieutenant Martin Withers, which would return to Ascension once Reeve had successfully completed the first aerial refuelling. The operations team calculated that some of the fuel would pass through five aircraft before being burned by the attack aircraft's Rolls-Royce Olympus engines.

Earlier on the flight-line, engineering chief Squadron Leader Mel James' team had found snags on both XM598 and XM607. It was a tough call, but at this point John Reeve elected to take XM598 as primary, as it was serviceable and functional prior to XM607's functions test at 1600hrs. Functionals, the sole purpose of checking the aircraft systems to validate the operational status were complete on XM607, both Vulcans were combat-readied and manoeuvred with considerable difficulty into position, edging out a C-130 and VC-10, ready for the mission.

At 1442hrs, an hour after the Victor briefing, Air Vice-Marshal George Chesworth received the execute order for *Black Buck 1* from John Curtiss at Northwood: 'Take-off at 2300hrs Zulu tonight, subject to refined timing with receipt of updated weather forecasting. Execute will be sent by flash.' Half an hour later the order came through. At 2100hrs a communication blackout commenced. V-bomber pilots, navigators, air electronics officers and air-to-air refuelling instructors sat listening on folding chairs, their leather flying boots immersed amongst discarded coffee cups, food wrappers, cigarette butts and empty packets on the red cinder earth. After Trevor Sitch explained the complex shape of the formation and refuelling plans, the crews synchronized their watches. After the refuelling plan brief, Squadron Leader Bill McQueen, Meteorological Officer, spoke. South-westerlies meant headwinds of up to 70 knots on the way down, but more significant was information that 20 to 40 degrees south, two cold fronts meant thunderstorms and turbulence during refuelling. As the briefing came to an end, Air Vice-Marshal Chesworth stood up to speak: 'This has never been done before; the eyes of the world are on you; there's a lot riding on this.'

Minutes later Chesworth and the air campaign team watched both Vulcan crews, wearing harnesses and Mae West lifejackets layered over thick immersion suits, walking in unison past a lengthy line of Victors towards their aircraft. In another line on the far side, the five-man crews of the K.2s disappeared through hatches. Now Chesworth privately worried whether the RAF's 'tin triangle' (Vulcan) upon which so much depended, would live up to its pre-war hype.

On the apron a snag was identified by AEO Flight Lieutenant Hugh Prior aboard XM607: their Dash-10 ECM pod was not functioning. The problem was diagnosed by RAF Honington specialist technician Corporal Webb as a tripped fuse on the X-band circuit board. Prior gave a thumbs up – they were still on. Webb scrambled out of the Vulcan and the aircraft's hatch was sealed shut, with the crew chief giving the final clearance.

At 2250hrs the Victors began to move out in line towards the runway in a sandstorm of dust. As just one aircraft at a time could align on the runway at once, the jets hauled themselves into the air at 60-second intervals between 2253hrs and 2308hrs. After take-off, the aircraft of each section closed up using speed differentials in the climb-out lane. A trombone pattern at the top-of-climb was incorporated to enable the three separate Red, White and Blue sections to join as one formation before proceeding down track. The noise changed dramatically to the familiar Vulcan 'howl' as John Reeve started rolling in XM598, then Martin Withers and his crew in XM607. But as Withers climbed away, Reeve's primary aircraft suffered a cabin pressure failure due to the rubber seal on the captain's 'direct vision' side-window (DV window). Unable to fix it, Reeve turned back to Wideawake four minutes after take-off; Withers now took the lead. The crew faced a 16hr flight sustained only by sandwiches and a flask of Nestlé coffee. On the upside, Vulcan XM607 had a better and more reliable bombing system than XM598.

Too heavily loaded for immediate landing, Reeve in XM598 burned off fuel at 20,000lb per hour, with the Vulcan's airbrakes out and undercarriage lowered to generate drag. Two hours and 15 minutes later the Vulcan touched down and rolled off the runway. After the shutdown checks and once everyone was out, there was a terse exchange with Alastair Montgomery, and technicians boarded XM598. The engineers' report dated 30 April revealed that John Reeve had shut his DV window too quickly when his slot appeared, trapping the seal. Blue Two had became unserviceable. The defective DV window was rectified in ten minutes by a technician. However, other technical problems on XM598 included intermittent intercom due to multiple headphone lead issues; variation in fuel consumption due to diode failure; and a fuse problem that caused a difficulty with the airbrake.

Black Buck 1 was still a 'go'. Withers moved across to XM598's vacant position in Blue Section, made up of three Victors. Twenty minutes later tankers trailed their centreline hose to identify any problems with refuelling equipment. Unfortunately, Squadron Leader Frank Milligan had a faulty hose drum unit (HDU) and pulled out of the armada; the airborne spare, Victor XH669, Blue Three (Reserve) captained by Flight Lieutenant Steve Biglands, replaced him as White Four in the outbound wave, leaving only one reserve tanker. The first and last tankers were separated by 85nm over the South Atlantic Ocean. With lights extinguished, the Victors' descent from 39,000ft to 29,000ft was more responsive and stable; then, using the tankers' HDU lights as an approach indicator, the four lead Victors of Red and White elements refuelled their respective tankers, taking on 49,100lb to 123,000lb, and departed for Ascension. On the return flight, each of the four tanker crews independently figured out that they were going to be critically short of fuel. One broke radio silence to air his concerns and notes were compared. Two Pan Am controllers at Wideawake guided them down without mishap. Each aircraft landed then pulled to the end of the runway and waited for the next. Their gauges showed that only 3,000lb of fuel remained in their tanks on landing: an indicator to Jerry Price that fuel consumption was much higher than forecast.

Avro Vulcan XM607 landing back at Wideawake airfield after completing *Black Buck 1*. (Crown Copyright, MOD)

Fuel misallocation

The complex refuelling routine continued after XM607's first specific air refuelling bracket one and three-quarter hours after take-off, Vulcan XM607 was refuelled twice by a separate tanker, Wing Commander Colin Seymour's Blue 1, which also departed the formation for Ascension. From Ascension to East Falkland was over eight hours. As the formation travelled, fuel was dispensed as if playing musical chairs: second bracket 1,700 miles south of Ascension, then bracket three at 2,600 miles.

Crew of XM607 (left to right): Flying Officer Pete Taylor; Flight Lieutenant Bob Wright; Flight Lieutenant Martin Withers; Flight Lieutenant Hugh Prior; Flight Lieutenant Gordon Graham. The sixth member of the crew is missing from the photo; he was Flight Lieutenant Dick Russell, the air-to-air refuelling instructor from the Victor OCU at RAF Marham. (Crown Copyright, MOD)

XM607 burnt 16,250lb of fuel an hour (4,000lb more than it should), due to the excessive take-off weight (210,000lb, rather than the normal 204,000lb), and the external Dash-10 under the starboard wing caused extra drag and added to the consumption. Despite having comparable combat service ceilings, the Vulcan's optimal cruising height was 40,000ft. The formation overall was at its most fuel-efficient when maintaining the Victors' optimal cruising altitude, so XM607 had to stay at 30,000ft to keep station, guzzling fuel on the long flight south until only two Victors remained from the original 15.

At 40° south located around the third refuelling bracket, against a dramatic backdrop of dazzling white flashes from an electrical storm, Steve Biglands' White Four was planned to take fuel from Squadron Leader Bob Tuxford's XL189 White Two, then escort Vulcan XM607 all the way south to the final refuelling before the attack. In appalling conditions, the hose began large oscillations as the two jets were hurled around volatile skies. Biglands physically fought to avoid ramming Tuxford's aircraft. The enormous lateral forces caused the tip of the 4in-thick refuelling probe to sheer off at the cast weakest point and the transfer was not completed. Tuxford's quick thinking on swapping roles saved *Black Buck 1* from being aborted. The three V-bombers pushed south, fuel being pumped from White Four through the long hose back into White Two before rendezvousing with the Vulcan. Biglands had given what fuel he could spare, retaining sufficient to make the six-hour flight back to Wideawake, as with the broken probe he could not be refuelled.

Tuxford's dilemma was whether his Victor's drogue was damaged, or if Biglands' probe had remained steadfast in his drogue too. He had to discover if they could continue so ran with the idea of a trial transfer to the Vulcan to prove that the system functioned. As the hose trailed out behind XL189, Withers closed in behind, with Dick Russell in the co-pilot's seat shining a torch into the drogue with no obvious problems. Russell, the Marham air-to-air refuelling instructor, made contact and the fuel began to flow into the Vulcan, some 5,000lb. Tuxford was satisfied that the kit wouldn't cause an abort as his Victor and the Vulcan continued south.

After the original fuel plan was dropped, there was an intense half-hour of rapid number-crunching, in a lively atmosphere that interspersed comic moments with the tension that arose from an awareness of the consequences of their decision – namely whether to refuel

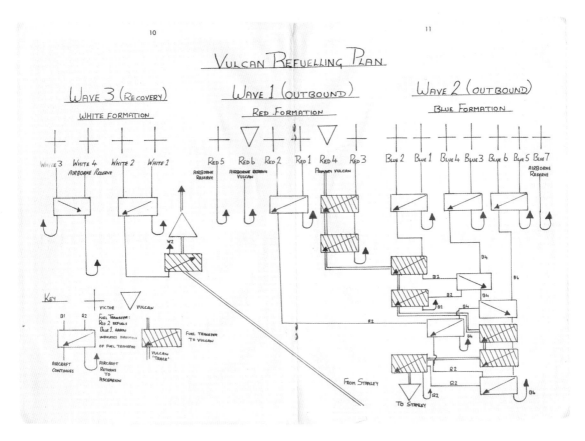

Hand-drawn refuelling plan for the Victors of No. 55 Squadron and No. 57 Squadron on *Black Buck 1*. (Courtesy of Royal Air Force Museum)

Martin Withers' Vulcan or splash down 460 miles south of Ascension Island. Ultimately they figured it out.

The final fuelling transfer at Bracket Four, about 500 miles north of the Falklands, commenced within minutes. The fuel was flowing from White Two into Vulcan XM607's tanks, then amber lights on the HDU flashed to break contact, but their probe remained connected and fuel still gushed into their tanks. Dick Russell heard Bob Tuxford in his headphones in a terse voice calling 'Blue Two break contact'. He had eaten into fuel reserves, in the deliberate and sombre knowledge that without an emergency tanker, his aircraft would run out of fuel some 500 nautical miles south of Ascension Island. Colin Seymour hours later flew to meet Tuxford, who was desperately short of fuel. Finding him over a thousand miles away, he performed the fuel transfer successfully, and disaster was averted.

Withers found himself 7,000lb short of what he expected. Dismissing Dick Russell's 'We should abort,' Martin Withers said to his crew 'We're short of fuel, but we've come this far, I'm not turning back now.' Vulcan XM607 was on its own. Three hundred miles from the target, Prior advised that everything that would transmit a signal should be immediately turned off, except for their intercom. Their descent at 2,000ft per minute had the adverse effect of icing up their pitot tube. As a result, the air speed indicator stopped working, which meant the instrumentation was wrong. Flying Officer Pete Taylor, who had swapped over with Russell, hauled back the stick to raise the nose and let the air speed drop off, then began their descent to 300ft, making doubly sure that the Argentine Westinghouse TPS-43 radar would not pick up the incoming Vulcan. Withers and Taylor were now reliant on navigator Flight Lieutenant Gordon Graham plotting their track using a northern hemisphere Mercator chart turned upside down to replicate the southern hemisphere!

Approaching the east–west runway at Port Stanley, XM607 was running in on a track of 235 degrees. As the range came down, the H2S radar was switched on. It had calibrated by 40 miles out but Flying Officer Bob Wright was unable to see any of the expected signs of returns on the CRT display from Mount Usborne, a mountain in the middle of East Falkland. With no hit on the mountain, the Vulcan was eased up to 500ft to widen the radar horizon, and within seconds Wright got a response. The nose was plunged down to get below Argentinian radar, but an early warning radar sweeping the south-west had Vulcan XM607 on its scope as the V-bomber accelerated.

Still wearing his thick rubber immersion suit, Martin Withers enjoys a post-ops beer with Group Captain Jeremy Price, Senior RAF Officer on Ascension (centre) and Air Vice Marshal George Chesworth from Northwood Headquarters. (Crown Copyright/ Ministry of Defence. Reproduced with kind permission of the Controller of Her Majesty's Stationery Office)

Approach to Stanley

On Sapper Hill (Cerro Zapador) on East Falkland south of Stanley, GADA 601 commander Lubin's Cardion TPS-44 Mk II A/O was positioned with a Skyguard fire-control radar. The TPS-44 was down on this occasion, but Vulcan XM607's approach was detected by the 3a Batería AA. Skyguard. Second Lieutenant Oscar Barri requested immediate permission from his battery chief to fire four of the unit's 12 Oerlikon 35/90 cannons. This was denied, owing to indecisiveness at the Information Control Centre in Stanley. Within seconds the blip had vanished, then caused disbelief by reappearing. Barri's experienced operator called out height, speed and range. The earlier negative reaction meant that Barri and his teams checked all aircraft movements around the islands for any early inbound flights. There were none; the signal was therefore regarded as hostile. Barri alerted Stanley, and Argentinian air defence system operators awaited orders. None came. The electronic jamming blinded Argentine communications, affecting radar, guns and the command centre at Stanley. Therefore there was no alarm, and the Vulcan would receive no welcome from AAA.

With the advantage of almost complete surprise, two miles short of Port Stanley airport's runway, the Vulcan's bombing computer calculated when the middle 'iron' bomb would detonate in the centre of the runway, and signalled bomb release. Within seconds the weapons were gone, but Martin Withers had to maintain a steady straight-and-level bombing course at nearly 400mph until all 21 bombs were clear of the aircraft. Inside, an amber light flashed 'bombs gone'. Within 20 seconds the string of bombs hit, angled south-westerly across Stanley airport runway. The first caught the edge of the tarmac, and a cone of concrete and hardcore 59ft wide and 22ft deep was vaporized by the explosion, while the earth below was heaved over the lip of the new crater. One hundred feet on and a quarter of a second later, the next bomb hit the ground and clawed out another chunk of the airfield, followed by the rest of the bombs in a rapid string of blasts.[4] From the epicentre of each blast, shockwaves rippled out, and instantly

4   Despite having received the information from a European Partner of the possible attack on May 1, there was a lack of adequate means to demarcate the runway. An attempt was made to organise a dummy runway using portable electrical equipment and lanterns but due to the lack of a correct lighting, an aircraft went off the runway on takeoff and the attempt was therefore abandoned.

a scorching red pressure wave swept violently through the control tower knocking out all communication equipment. Major Alberto Iannariello, inside, was slammed onto the floor and rendered unconscious. Outside, Hector Bordon and Guillermo Garcia, both young Argentinian Air Force conscripts, together with Raul Romero of the Batallón de Antiaere Infanteria Marina, lay dead: the first casualties of the Falklands conflict.

Argentine radar operators were able to raise the alarm after the jamming faded and frantically contacted Argentina. At 0940hrs local time on 1 May, on the Argentine east coast, some three hours behind, the command-and-control centre at Río Gallegos received word that a British Vulcan bomber had made a single strike against Stanley airport. A pair of Grupo 8 Mirage IIIEAs on high alert were scrambled. Climbing to 39,000ft on a route towards the Falklands, each was armed with a pair of 30mm DEFA 552 cannon and French Matra R.500 Magic short-range air-to-air missiles, with an operational range of 6.2 miles. Staying high and at their optimum cruising speed, they believed they held the advantage over the defenceless bomber as they flew towards their embattled comrades.

Returning to Stanley airfield after an Islander flight from Volunteer Point, November 1983. A pair of 29 Squadron Phantoms are in the foreground, while soft-walled shelters are being erected to form hangars. (Dennis Gooch/Getty Images)

Vulcan B.2/*Black Buck 1* attack on Port Stanley airfield, 30 April–1 May 1982

On the night of 30 April/1 May 1982, Flight Lieutenant Martin Withers stepped into the lead on the outbound flight for *Black Buck 1*, and made the first combat flight in an Avro Vulcan B.2 bomber. Squadron Leader Bob Tuxford flying Victor (White 2) was tasked to refuel the Vulcan (Blue 2) and, after changing roles, continued south. Both Withers and Tuxford flew to the last fuel bracket. Tuxford refuelled the Vulcan which drained his own fuel reserves. Now alone, Withers flew on to the Falklands, making his approach at low level, dropping to 300ft before climbing to 1,000ft for the bomb run 40 miles from his main target – Port Stanley airport.

The approach was monitored by GADA 601 3a Batería Skyguard radar operators on Sapper Hill. Coordinates were keyed into the computer system and four Oerlikon 35mm cannons tracked the threat. Their fire mission against the aircraft was denied by their command centre.

To verify their position, Vulcan XM607 H2S Mk 9 radar eventually locked onto the peak of Mount Usborne, 33 miles west of Stanley, before the automated bombing control system was engaged. Withers made the final approach at 10,000ft, with an airspeed of 330 knots (610 km/h). GADA 601 3a Batería Skyguard radar operators still had XM607 on their screen. Notifying command centre for a second time, a fire mission was refused as it could be a friendly Hercules C-130 or P-2 Neptune. As Argentinian commanders dithered, the Vulcan's DASH-10 pod was switched on. At 4 miles to the target aircrafts, ECM was blanking out all Argentinian air defence.

At 2 miles, at an angle of 35°, the automated bomb release dropped 21 bombs at short intervals. Withers put the Vulcan into a 60-degree bank to the left, subjecting the crew to 2 g (20 m/s2), twice the force of gravity, as they made their escape. Travelling at 440mph, Vulcan XM607 was 3 miles away when the first bomb exploded. As concrete was ripped up on the runway, the remaining 20 bombs impacted near troops under canvas. Their wooden barricades proved useless against the shock waves and there were deaths. Outside Stanley harbour, waiting to enter, *Río Carcaraña*, carrying GADA 101's Batería B equipment and transport, was hit by the shock waves and swung like a pendulum until its crew managed to stabilize it. A rapid move was made to San Carlos for off-loading.

Withers headed nearly due north to a planned rendezvous with a Victor off the Brazilian coast, adjacent to Rio de Janeiro. Rules of Engagement meant a live fire ban in a radius around the British Task Force as the RAF Vulcan XM607 was routed nearby. Its crew signalled the code word 'superfuse' indicating a successful attack at 0746Z which was picked up by HMS *Hermes*. The illustration shows Vulcan B.2, mid air in cloud cover, flying away from the target, with an explosion in the background.

Overflying Stanley airfield in a Britten-Norman Islander, November 1983. Two C-130 Hercules aircraft with refuelling probes stand on the apron. The air traffic control tower has been rebuilt, and expansion is in progress. (Dennis Gooch/Getty Images)

When within range of the AN/TPS-44 radar both pilots tried to contact the controller but were unable to.[5] Without being vectored by ground controllers informed by this radar, with its range of 460 miles, the jets' Thomson-CSF Cyrano II radar systems with their 25-mile range were never going to pick up the bogie. Realizing their hopeless predicament, both returned to Río Gallegos. The Grupo 8 pilots had hoped to humble the RAF by destroying their Vulcan using speed and modern weaponry but had failed in their attempt.

Unaware of the threat out over the South Atlantic, on board Vulcan XM607 at 0746Z the codeword 'Superfuse' was relayed to base, signifying the success of the attack. As Martin Withers returned across the South Atlantic, he was shocked that they had emerged safely. Because of the weather conditions and the higher than planned fuel consumption, Vulcan XM607 was further south and an hour later than planned. With less than 8,000lb of fuel spread around the Vulcan's 14 tanks, they were close to running on fumes when Victor navigator Chris Morffew guided Barry Neal through a perfectly executed 210-degree turn, rolling out 3 miles dead ahead of the Vulcan with their hose trailing. For Withers and his crew it was deliverance. The connection was good and a successful transfer was completed. XM607 touched down at 1452Z to complete a 15hrs and 5mins combat mission on what was (at the time) the longest mission ever flown by any aircraft of British military aviation. Neal in Victor XH672, with a Nimrod part of the recovery section, returned after 5hrs 40mins. Behind the scenes, the White House Situation Room heard from a British Ministry of Defence official that substantial damage had been inflicted.

At Port Stanley

During April Stanley airport had been christened BAM Malvinas by Vice Commodore Wilson Pedrozo, with all his staff singing the Argentine national anthem in front of a flagpole flying the national flag. The island had been supplied by the C-130 Hercules of I 'El Palomar' *Brigada Aérea* (1st Air Brigade 'El Palomar'), along with Boeing 737 flights by the state commercial airline, Aerolíneas Argentinas, between 2 and 29 April. To keep this air bridge open, Argentine Energy Company YPF supplied barrels of JP-1 and JP-4 aviation fuel. Juan Carlos Pellegrini, president of Aerolíneas Argentinas, had supplied two Boeing 737-200s for the role: maintenance personnel having stripped out passenger seats, carpets and linings to reduce their basic empty weight, so that each aircraft could transport a minimum of 10 tons to BAM Malvinas. 'The greatest difficulty of the entire operation was to approach, land and brake almost 46 tons that touched about 135 knots on the short runway,' said former airline pilot César Gatti.

The following tables show the supplies flown to Port Stanley by both C-130s and 737s during April 1982.

---

5   The pilots in the Mirage IIIEAs had not been given new radio frequencies for in flight that enabled them to speak with radar operators/controllers on the Falklands.

I 'El Palomar' Brigada Aérea supplies pre-*Black Buck* 1			
Hours flown	No. of landings	Personnel	Equipment
1,620	397	9,215	5,008 tons

Aerolíneas Argentinas flights, Boeing 737 LV-JTD and LV-LEB				
Flights	Scheduled flights	No. of landings	Personnel	Equipment
20–24 April from Río Gallegos	43	41	4,100	Not known
25–27 April from Comodoro Rivadavia	29	29	1,400	160 tons
25–27 April from Río Gallegos	20	19	1,000	110 tons

Withers' single hit dug a great hole in the runway structure. When the debris and shrapnel was cleared, the Argentinians filled the crater with aggregate from the quarry to allow the airfield to be used by transport aircraft. However, the infill materials were not blended properly to give a consistent result, and the runway's load-bearing capacity was reduced still further. *Black Buck 1*'s single crater halted the 737 flights.

The Argentinians recorded:

On 1 May 1982: Twenty-one bombs fell from a Vulcan: Destroyed two trucks and a bulldozer. On the runway, the devastating effect of the explosive had opened a crater 18m [59ft] in diameter and 6.80m [22.3] in depth. The Air Bridge from mainland Argentina was briefly halted and the crater filled in and paved again. That is why only the scattered debris was removed, the edges were smoothed and, with one section of the runway reduced in width, so our missions continued.

Anti-aircraft defences meant British reconnaissance jets had to fly high at an estimated 20,000ft to photograph. Maiorano's men simulated three blast craters on the runway which could be easily removed then replaced in the exact same position before the arrival of each transport aircraft.

On 6 May, Commander Alfredo Abelardo of I 'El Palomar' Brigada Aérea watched the first C-130 depart from Comodoro Rivadavia since Withers' raid. Clear of the coast, the olive-and-brown Hercules dropped to 32ft flying at 245mph over the sea to a designated point, to make a 'dark' approach onto the runway at 81mph and brake in less than 2,000ft. With its cargo bay doors already open, unloading commenced at the opposite end of the runway with all four engines running for a tactical take-off. The unarmed, unescorted C-130s continued to resupply Argentine forces on the Falkland Islands until 13 June using short take-off and landing (STOL) together with parachute resupplies of 19 tons over the airport. Their nightly supply sorties into Stanley would gain the respect of many British aircrew.

I 'El Palomar' Brigada Aérea supplies post-*Black Buck* 1					
Sorties	Scheduled flights	Landings	Air drops	CASEVAC	Cargo
6 May – 13 June	74	31	6	264	434 tons

Other Argentine aircraft had also flown in troops and supplies until *Black Buck 1*: the last Argentinian Air Force F-28 passenger/cargo flights arrived at midnight on 29 April, and their Fokker F-27 Friendship fleet would not return either. However, the Aviación Naval Argentina (Argentine Naval Aviation) Fokker F-28 and Lockheed Electra continued flying into BAM Malvinas from mainland Argentina after *Black Buck 1*. The final supply flight by C-130, carrying 155mm shells, touched down shortly before midnight on 13 June before the Argentine forces surrendered on 14 June. From 2 April official figures show that 23,428 troops were landed onto the Malvinas; based on figures supplied for aircraft landing at BAM Malvinas, 21,808 of these were air lifted onto the island.

Fuerza Aérea Argentina Escuadrón II Fokker F-28				
Flights	Hours flown	Landings	Personnel	Equipment
2–29 April	1,150	228	5,570	816 tons

Fuerza Aérea Argentina Escuadrón IV del Grupo 1 de Transporte Fokker F-27			
Flights	Landings	Personnel	Cargo
2–29 April	309	Not Specified	Not Specified

Aviación Naval Argentina Fokker F-28 and Lockheed Electra			
Flights	Landings	Personnel	Equipment
2–30 April	58	903	361 tons
1 May – 14 June	12	Not specified	500 tons

The Sea Harrier follows up

Minutes after the Mirage IIIEAs returned to base, 12 Sea Harriers of No. 800 Squadron launched from HMS *Hermes* at 0748hrs to follow up the Vulcan mission. Each was armed with a combination of 1,000lb iron bombs fused to airburst or parachute-retarded 1,000lb bombs. The armourers fitted fuses to airburst at 1.5m (4.9ft) in the air instead of on contact with the ground, meaning that the burst and shock wave from the explosion and the shell fragments were distributed more evenly over a wider area. Their 1,000lb bombs were fitted with impact or delayed fuses, BL755 cluster bombs, which contained a further 147 smaller bomblets, which would pop open after release from the aircraft scattering anti-personnel munitions. The three sections from No. 800 Naval Air Squadron attacked the airport at Stanley and the Goose Green airfield. Red Section flew in from the east, dropping 12 1,000lb bombs to soften up the mixed GADA 602 and GADA 601 Batería B air defence systems that provided cover for the airport site, as Black Section, led by squadron chief Lieutenant Commander Andy Auld, darted in from the north-west. The five Black Section jets dropped retarded bombs, adding to the damage left by the Vulcan. Cluster bombs were also released over the airport site.

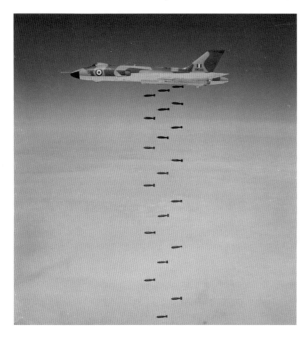

Vulcan B2 XM599 of No. 35 Squadron releases a full bomb load of 21 1,000lb bombs in the 1960s. (Andrew D. Bird Collection

Most of the Sea Harriers approached their targets at a height of 5–15ft off the ground, giving a new meaning to the term 'daisy-cutters'. The select band of Argentine operators of 602 GADA had to overcome the seconds-robbing mystique and allure of the British V/STOL jet: 'The first time I saw a Harrier jump jet, I was so fascinated momentarily staring, and that's fatal,' said one veteran defender at BAM Malvinas. However, at Sapper Hill, 6.3 miles south-west of Stanley airport, the optical aimer First Sergeant Jorge Zelaya got a contact, and fired a Roland SAM at one of five Sea Harriers that was attacking the airport, without result. During that

Overall view of Wideawake airfield on Ascension with Nimrod, Victors, Hercules, Sea Harriers, Chinook and VC-10. (Andrew D. Bird Collection)

same attack, Corporal Andrés Momo, using the optical mode, fired two Tigercat missiles at the same targets without success. One Tigercat missile weaved off course, crashing into the water 100yd from the Empresa Líneas Marítimas Argentinas (ELMA) freighter *Formosa*. As 20mm and 30mm AAA shells sprayed over the site up to a height of 1,000ft, two radar-controlled Oerlikon 20mm cannons tracked attacking Sea Harriers. As smoke from a fuel dump and Andy Auld's cluster bombs drifted east, Flight Lieutenant David Morgan in ZA192 had a Britten-Norman Islander firmly in his sights and released three cluster bombs. Suddenly there was an explosion. An Oerlikon firing 20mm cannon shells punched a hole 6in across in his Harrier's fin and tail plane. He and his colleagues dispensed their ordnance from all 12 jets, then sped towards the carrier. The Sea Harriers suffered no losses. The BBC's Brian Hanrahan, reporting from *Hermes*, announced on air that he could not give the number of Sea Harriers involved: 'But I counted them all out, and I counted them all back.'

Lieutenant Commander Neill Thomas flew high across Stanley airport with a single Vinten F.95 camera mounted on a Sea Harrier taking photographs from 20,000ft. *Black Buck 1* was judged a success by the slenderest of margins; a few military staff had been sceptical about the claims that Beetham had made.[6] The raid proved that British airmen had not lost the courage, élan, and verve that their predecessors had shown. With the use of the Vulcan judged to be a success, it was decided to mount a second raid. A revision to Waddington's command structure saw Squadron Leader Anthony Wright of No. 50 Squadron in Baldwin's operations team relocate to Northwood as the designated Vulcan expert, working side by side with a Harrier and a Victor expert.

Later that same morning, Woodward detached destroyer HMS *Glamorgan* and the frigates HMS *Alacrity* and HMS *Arrow* to bombarded Argentine positions. The trio arrived on station at 1600Z and, despite Northwood's disapproval of the plan fearing the loss of a guided-missile destroyer, *Glamorgan*'s guns blasted Sapper Hill west of the capital. One vehicle was disabled but neither the blast nor shrapnel affected either the AN/TPS-44 or the Skyguard radar position. At 1830hrs (1530 local time) Brigadier Ernesto Crespo's Fuerza

6   One hour after the Sea Harrier raid a Pucará A-513 transiting to Darwin piloted by Lieutenant Ramon Brest made an emergency landing. It would not fly again.

KEY

Harrier 1

Harrier 2

Vulcan

8

7

12

10

11

9

Black Buck 1

AAA anti-aircraft guns 35mm 120mm

Radar AAA

SAM sites

Stanley Airport Defence

EVENTS

1 Vulcan flying at 10,000ft over Stanley releases bombs two miles before Stanley runway, continues then turns 60 degrees to port.

2 0700hrs. Sea Harriers from Red and Black Sections make landfall at Macbride Head, the most north-easterly point of the Falkland Islands.

3 Red and Black Sections fly from Macbride Head to Volunteer Point (eight miles at 550mph) in 52 seconds.

4 Red and Black Sections split up at Volunteer Point. Red Section then continues to the Stanley airport entry point.

5 0701hrs. Black Section crosses Berkeley Sound at low altitude.

6 0701hrs. Red Section crosses Berkeley Sound to Tussac Island at an altitude of a few feet.

7 0701hrs. An Argentinian civilian amateur radio-operator near Black Point (one of a number of substitute observers who were replaced by the military from May 1982) alerts the Stanley command centre.

8 0702hrs. Black Section flies over Cochon Island through the mountain pass between Mount Low and Beagle Ridge, over Blanco Bay into Stanley airport at between 5 to 15ft and drops ordnance and strafes positions.

9 Slightly ahead of Black Section, Red Section flies over Tussac Island into Stanley airport and, within seven seconds, strafes positions using ADEN 30mm cannons, drops cluster bombs and 1,000lb bombs.

10 Black Section's David Morgan turns hard left into Stanley airport, passing between Kelly Rocks and Tussock Islands as Oerlikon 35/90 AAA defence battery opens fire.

11 Argentine soldiers open fire with small arms, as the Harrier flies below sand-dune height. As it crosses back over, Morgan uses the jet wash to flatten soldiers and increases altitude to 150ft and drops three cluster bombs on the airfield. A cannon shell fired by Oerlikon 35/90 AAA hits the tail of the Harrier.

12 Morgan exits over Canopus Hill then turns east to rendezvous with Navy carriers.

Aérea Argentina launched a response against the British from the mainland to what was believed to be a full-scale landing. Soon the trio came under attack by three Israeli-built Dagger jets (straight copy of the Mirage) of Grupo 6; *Glamorgan* fired a Seacat missile, *Arrow* opened fire with 20mm cannon and *Alacrity* with a single GMPG. But two 500lb bombs exploded alongside *Glamorgan*, causing minor underwater damage. One strafed *Arrow* causing the Tasks Force's first naval casualty. Two days later, in an attempt to decrease the effects of persistent naval shelling as much as possible, the AN/TPS-44 system moved to a site near Stanley airport (BAM Malvinas), enabling a link firstly with the Fuerza Aérea Argentina radar and then by radio and telephone line to Government House.

The *Belgrano* sinking and its consequences

The Argentinian Navy remained a significant threat to the British task force. The two most powerful groups were centred on two large warships. The cruiser ARA General Belgrano was a former World War II US Navy light cruiser, and was escorted by two destroyers, equally vintage but upgraded with Exocet missiles. Formerly the British HMS *Venerable*, the aircraft carrier ARA *Veinticinco de Mayo* was escorted by two modern and Exocet-equipped Type 42 destroyers, and operated jets and ex-US Navy piston-engined Grumman S-2 Tracker surveillance aircraft. These were fitted with a centrally mounted retractable radome for AN/APS-38 radar and a Magnetic Anomaly Detector (MAD) AN/ASQ-8 mounted on an extendable rear-mounted boom. S-2 Trackers had nine hours' endurance.

ARA *Veinticinco de Mayo* had three Trackers on board when it formed part of a defensive perimeter around the Malvinas. The carrier was deployed in a task force 200 miles north of the islands, with ARA *General Belgrano* and its escorts to the south. Surveillance and anti-submarine warfare patrols were continually flown, six-hour missions flying as far as 100 miles from the carrier to drop sonobuoys and use their surface-search radars. They also used electromagnetic sensors to listen for radio signals sent to or from British submarines. HMS *Splendid* was indeed chasing down ARA *Veinticinco de Mayo*, but had lingering boiler problems, which meant that the submarine could not reach its maximum speed. As the carrier zig-zagged through shallower waters, its aircraft detected what they thought was HMS *Splendid*, and the Trackers attacked with Mk 44 torpedoes and Mk 54 depth charges. Despite the Argentinian defences, *Splendid* closed the distance by 3 May, and was close enough to make visual contact.

In London, the War Cabinet received secret intercepts from Chilean intelligence services revealing orders from the Argentine Junta to ARA *General Belgrano* were to sink a [British] carrier. The War Cabinet briefed at Chequers by Sir Terence Lewin, Admiral of the Fleet, took the decision to sink the *Belgrano*. The order was flashed through Northwood to the submarine HMS *Conqueror*. Commander Chris Wreford-Brown, the captain, fired two non-guided torpedoes. At 1457hrs local time on 2 May, the torpedos blew off the ship's bow when it was outside the 200-mile exclusion zone and steaming away from the islands. It was militarily 'one of the easiest decisions of the war' but resulted in the loss of 323 Argentinian sailors. Although *Neptune* 2-P-111 established contact at 0955hrs on 3 May with one of 15 scattered inflatable life rafts, its fuel status then forced a return to Río Grande. In Buenos Aires in the subsequent hours, there was stunned silence. In a communiqué issued later on the

Northwood, Middlesex, 12 April. Left to right: Vice Admiral Peter Herbert, Flag Officer Submarines; Major General Jeremy Moore, Major General Royal Marines; Admiral Sir John Fieldhouse, Commander-in-Chief Fleet; Vice Admiral David Halifax, Chief of Staff to Civic Fleet; Air Marshal Sir John Curtiss, Air-Officer-Commanding 18 Group, Rear Admiral Peter Hammersley (Andrew D. Bird Collection)

3 May, the Argentines confirmed the sinking and the military Junta ordered that all sea transport sailing across to the islands be halted immediately. After this date, the Argentine fleet remained in port and played no major role in the rest of the conflict. This was the clincher, effectively imposing sea denial and forcing Argentina's forces to use only air transport to supply the islands with personnel, equipment, weaponry and supplies. It meant that the Argentinian Navy could not deploy their carrier-borne aircraft, forcing them to operate from land bases at the limit of their endurance. Withers' single bomb on the Port Stanley runway, and the sinking of the *General Belgrano*, had combined to make Argentina's logistical position difficult.

Black Buck 2

Preparations were underway at Wideawake for the next raid, and the pace of activity was rapid. To help keep the Vulcans airborne, spares arrived on an ex-RAF Belfast transport aircraft chartered from Heavy Lift Cargo Airline. With the movement of many tons of explosives around the base becoming a regular occurrence, a C-130 Hercules landed at Ascension with RAF Type S Weapon Trollies on board ready for use. Further ordnance arrived at 2340hrs on 2 May aboard

Air Chief Marshal of the RAF Sir Michael Beetham was nearing retirement when the Argentine forces invaded the Falkland Islands on 2 April 1982. Believing from the outset that the RAF should make a direct operational contribution with an attack on Stanley airport, he realized that such an attack was an especially demanding undertaking for his Vulcan bomber and Victor tanker crews but he pushed for it in the face of some scepticism in Whitehall. (Andrew D. Bird Collection)

a C-130 Hercules: another full load of 21 1,000lb bombs and fuses on pallets. The fuses were taken to Bomb Dump A, an hour and a quarter round trip from Wideawake. The bombs on their carriers were unloaded and left on pallets forward of the C-130 apron, and a Pan Am crane was hired to lift the bomb load onto the weapons trollies, on which they could be moved easily and safely. At 0431hrs the tailfins were fitted and the bombs were secure in the aircraft's bomb bay by 0520hrs on 3 May.

A signal arrived from Northwood to alter the fuse settings as the attack altitude was raised to 16,000ft to counter the SAM missile threat. A combination of the seven pre-set fuse settings was used to optimize the effect against its intended target for the second mission. Armourers from RAF Kinloss completed changing these fuse settings underneath XM598 and XM607 by 1130hrs that morning. At 1300hrs another 21 1,000lb bombs arrived by air to replenish the base's bomb store – unusually, a VC-10 from RAF Brize Norton conducted this flight. Pan Am again provided the crane to offload onto trollies. On the fourth day of Vulcan operations, 3 May, the campaign objective remained the same: disable the Stanley airport runway to render it unusable for fast jets.

Northwood headquarters gave the order for another Vulcan sortie. Pan Am air traffic controllers, using call-sign 'Red Rag Control', had two inbound aircraft from Banjul, Gambia, so there was an adjustment to the mission planning. Wing Commander Peter Squires in Harrier GR.3 XV789 fitted with two 330-gallon ferry tanks, accompanied by Squadron Leader Dave Foulger, Officer Commanding 232 Operational Conversion Unit, in Victor tanker XM715, both landed at 2215hrs. Squires had been in the cockpit for nine hours. Half an hour afterwards there was a communications blackout. Crews were briefed. By 2345hrs both Vulcans were taxiing out for take-off. On the first refuelling bracket John Reeve in Vulcan XM607 failed to give the coded signal for identification; Montgomery gave him a reminder, before XM598 returned to Wideawake. After flying the identical route to the previous *Black Buck 1*, again refuelled by 11 Victor K.2s, at 0520hrs on 4 May John Reeve's Vulcan dropped 21 1,000lb bombs from an altitude of 16,000ft to avoid the AAA and SAMs.

None of the bombs found the target, although the trail of bombs nearly reached the western corner of the runway. Arguably more damage had been inflicted by naval gunfire that day, when earlier an all-metal Short Sc.7 Skyvan (PA-54) light transport aircraft in an

A mixture of Sea Harriers, Harrier GR.3s and Sea King helicopters on the crowded deck of HMS *Hermes* during the Falklands campaign. (Andrew D. Bird Collection)

airport hangar had been hit by shells. The fins were repaired, and then the PA-54 was flown to Stanley racecourse. During the landing its front landing gear broke and the Skyvan stayed on site.

The Argentinians noted:

The Vulcan arrived again on 4 May but their aim was woeful. The Royal Navy's bombardment was an annoying custom because of their accuracy. Their shells left craters of various sizes, scattered debris and affected facilities on the airport. On each occasion, the runway was cleared, patched and repaired, but all this meant an intensive use of the material that, added to the unfavourable weather conditions, caused constant damage.

With five Victors in the recovery wave, Reeve landed at 1533hrs. He used extra power on taxiing, causing dust and gravel to be drawn into the air intakes of nearby Victor XL233. Technicians servicing the Vulcan reported a dysfunctional pressurization on the Red Steer tail warning radar along with the standby artificial horizon. Webb informed Westinghouse that the ALQ-101-10 ECM pod on XM607 was unserviceable too. The strain of operations was beginning to tell on the ageing aircraft.

The loss of the *General Belgrano* initially had been a severe psychological blow to the Argentines, and continued employment of Vulcan bombers from Ascension Island meant sentiment was running high in favour of a strike against the British Task Force. On 4 May, at 1100hrs local time, two land-based Argentine Navy Super Étendard fighter-bombers, flown by Capitán de Navío (Captain) Augusto Bedacarratz with wingman Lieutenant Armando Mayora, hit HMS *Sheffield* from 20 miles out with an AM.39 Exocet anti-ship missile. HMS *Glasgow* detected an Exocet missile fired at the Task Force and warned the fleet. However *Sheffield* failed to receive the warning. The frigate would sink under tow six days later. This was a shock and an immediate cause for concern: if one Exocet could get through the British defences, there was no reason why others should not. The tactic used by the Argentines flying Étendards meant the Sea Dart missile system was unreliable. Another gap in defence was Airborne Early Warning (AEW) aircraft, making the Task Force reliant on shipborne air search. The British Air Attaché in Washington had already informally requested information on Grumman AEW aircraft. Caspar Weinberger informed the British Embassy that there were Grumman E–2Bs in the US Navy Reserve.[7]

These Super Étendards had been guided by an Argentinian Lockheed SP-2H Neptune AEW, which detected *Sheffield* 85 miles south of Port Stanley. Onboard operators then passed its location and bearing to intercept. The Task Force was at risk of losing ships to Exocet-equipped aircraft guided either by Argentina's two remaining SP-2H Neptunes, before their withdrawal,[8] or by the Falklands-based AN/TPS-43/44 radar. This long-range

7   Central Intelligence Agency, Office of the Director of Central Intelligence, Job 89B00224R

8   Neptune SP-111 withdrew to Comandante Espora on 12 May, never to return. Three days later, SP-112 did the same, although it returned to Río Grande on the 26th then returned to the conflict on 4 June to fly its final mission. Its radar and electronic countermeasures equipment were no longer reliable as the US trade embargo meant that components could not be replaced. This was a huge loss to the Argentine combat capabilities; the gap was covered with their S-2E Trackers for a short period.

radar could replicate the Neptunes' role, to direct aircraft to strike the Task Force, and warn their pilots of Sea Harrier patrols, but most disturbing was that it had the capability to guide Exocet missiles. After hearing this, Curtiss ordered a tactics review. The RAF community on Ascension that evening heard of the loss of *Sheffield* and of Lieutenant Nick Taylor, killed in a Sea Harrier raid against targets on Goose Green airfield, which somewhat dampened the atmosphere.[9]

Air staff continued to oversee the feasibility studies to widen the Vulcan's capabilities to launch the AS.37 Martel with chaff dispensers in the bomb bay for self-defence, or to perform a combined mission carrying Martel to target the radars and a full bomb load to hit the runway again. While examining the possibilities, the RAF also looked at fitting heat-seeking AIM-9 Sidewinders for self-defence, and at fitting an AN/AVQ-23E Pave Spike laser target designator pod, designed to improve daylight, visual-conditions attack capabilities. The lack of experience with Pave Spike meant that the RAF opted to use a hand-held ground homing system. Also, the RAF's AN/AVQ-23E being a 'first-generation' targeting laser, Pave Spike could not 'see' in the dark. Trials went ahead on GBU-16 Paveway II Mk 83 at Waddington, with three laser-guided bombs carried in the bomb bay on launch trails at Jurby Head range. Successful launches saw the air and ground parties refine the procedures should further action within the conflict be required.

A French AM39 Exocet anti-ship missile on the wing of a Super Étendard fighter-bomber. Its mere presence affected much of the strategic and tactical thinking of British commanders, leading to a narrative of three British Special Forces operations to destroy the missiles on Argentine soil which were all aborted. (Photo by Jean-Claude FRANCOLON/Gamma-Rapho via Getty Images)

Vulcans fitted with improvised pylon for AS.37 Martel	
Serial No.	AS.37 Martel
XL391	•
XM597	•
XM607	•
XM612	•

Post-strike analysis of *Black Buck 2* was not immediately possible, as weather disrupted missions and the Sea Harriers remained on their carriers. When the weather cleared enough for a Sea Harrier to launch and bring back images, and when the film was developed, the results showed that none had hit the target. However, the craters near the end of the runway prevented any extension at the western end of the runway to make it safe for use by fast jets. C-130 Hercules, Fokker F-28 and Lockheed Electra aircraft were still able to use the runway.

In Middlesex, Anthony Wright heard frustratingly that none of the *Black Buck 2* 'dumb' bombs dropped had hit the target and that they had only caused damage to airfield facilities and life-changing injuries to two Argentine conscripts, while the task of getting more than one bomb on the runway remained unfulfilled. It drew great media focus, with armchair

9   Lieutenant Nick Taylor of No. 800 Squadron in aircraft XZ450 was hit by shells from two Oerlikon 35/90 cannons hooked up to Skyguard. He was still strapped into his ejector seat when recovered and buried with military honours by the Argentines near the airstrip. His aircraft, 'Five-Zero' XZ450, was the first Sea Harrier to fly on 20 August 1978.

'Nose Hangar' at the US Air Force base, Wideawake. Nearest aircraft (left to right): a Douglas A-20 Havoc with a pair of Bell P-39 Airacobras either side. In the hangar, a North American B-25 Mitchell (later used by No. 139 Wing RAF) with another Airacobras. A B-25 Mitchell sits on the apron.

OPPOSITE
Super Étendard 3-A-210 (s.0760) received on 9 December 1982. The jet is about to launch on the deck of the ARA *Veinticinco de Mayo* in April 1983. The aircraft crashed on 1 August 1989 on a low-level exercise near Monte Hermoso. (Photo by Luis Rosendo/Heritage Images via Getty Images)

critics and journalists implying that the RAF bomber crews had lost their skills in the nuclear age. Another raid was proposed for Thursday 6 May.

On Ascension the weather intervened on the 6th, so there could be no immediate sortie. However, the Vulcans anyway required maintenance before another mission. Red Steer spares arrived from Britain, to repair the tail radar that would not function through a 15-hour flight. A new Dash-10 ECM pod for XM607 was unpackaged and fitted. Red Steer, located at the tip of a Vulcan's tailcone, would continually require replacement during the Operation *Corporate* missions.

Group Captain Jerry Price received orders from Air Commander John Curtiss that both Vulcans were to return to Waddington. XM598 still had its original bomb load on board, so the Pan Am crane was again booked for 1600hrs on 7 May. The standby artificial horizon on XM607 was changed but the system then went down. The Vulcan was moved onto the apron ready for departure, but the aircraft had no hydraulic power pack unit for its brakes due to lack of charge. The problem was sorted by 1600hrs, when XM598's bomb load was removed and transferred to the bomb dump. The ECM pod remained on the aircraft as it was not up to current threat requirements and needed an update at Waddington. XM598's crew briefing took place at 1700hrs but the Vulcan could not be moved as its tug was employed towing trolleys with aircraft bombs. Instead, a Victor tanker's tug was borrowed – and the departure was again thwarted, as at 1715hrs the tow bar broke on the tug that was to move XM598, and the aircraft's nose wheel fell 4in into a rut in the tarmac. Price raged at the problem. Fortunately, Bill Bryden saved the day, taking Price into his office and quietly emphasizing that the pilot would be able to move the Vulcan. The road behind the apron was sealed off in preparation. John Reeve powered up XM598, throwing up clouds of dust and grit when the Vulcan moved out of the rut onto the apron. Shortly after 1800hrs, XM598 and XM607 taxied out with their accompanying Victors, with a planned stop at Banjul, Gambia, for the Victors as the Vulcans headed for Waddington. Once the USAF Support Unit on Wideawake had welded on a new tow bar, the tug was back in business.

Prior to *Black Buck 3* Captain Bob McQueen, Commander of British Forces Support Unit, had ordered the armourers to check if the stock of bomb fuses was adequate or if further supplies were required. On site, 57 Ferranti Type No. 947 tail fuses were available, with a delay variable between instant, milliseconds, or a few seconds. The No. 79 fuse, a mechanical, fork-armed, tail, chemical-delay, pistol (fuse) had longer nominal delay times. Of these, there were eight 30-minute fuses, as well as eight one-hour, nine six-hour, and six 36-hour fuses; fortunately, the delay times in hours were included as a suffix of the pistol number. There were enough for one aircraft, so a resupply was required.

The first anti-radar attempts

Black Buck 3 had been planned for 13 May, a historical date in the annals of the RAF, for that was when Wing Commander Guy Gibson and his crews of No. 617 Squadron had flown Operation *Chastise* nearly 40 years earlier. It was to be the last anti-runway mission using iron bombs, but would also attempt to destroy an Argentinian radar with a Martel missile. However, the arrival of the replacement Vulcans from Britain was delayed; Squadron Leader Bill Berrin, the duty night operations officer at Wideawake, finally received the signal at 0850hrs on 13 May to prepare to receive two Vulcans for the mission, with their estimated time of arrival initially 2100hrs, then 0300hrs on 14 May.

At 0045hrs another signal was received at Red Rag Control: the ETA was now 0200hrs, one hour earlier. But only one Vulcan was inbound to Ascension, piloted by John Reeve. XM612 touched down with a functioning Dash-10

ECM pod, an AS.37 Martel and a bomb bay laden with the remains of a 1,000lb bombload. After refuelling on the outbound flight, XM612's fuel consumption was slightly higher than originally calculated due to the payload and external stores, so Reeve had little alternative but to lighten the load, manually jettisoning the bomb load into the sea. Except that when released, five of the seven bombs on the centre bomb carrier snagged, failing to drop. Once XM612 was on the ground, the Ascension base commander Lieutenant Colonel Bill Bryden ordered the Vulcan to be moved to the end of Runway One-Four to remove the bomb load. 'We can spare the last three thousand feet of the runway should they detonate,' noted Bryden.

The bomb offloading was completed by 1030hrs on 14 May, and XM612 was towed onto the apron. However, several other defects needed rectifying. Problems with the central carrier persisted, as did issues with the Carousel inertial navigation system. The aircraft was declared unserviceable, and *Black Buck 3* was scrubbed. During a 'management briefing' regarding Vulcan operations *Black Buck 3* was rescheduled for the weekend of 15/16 May.

Task Force Commander Admiral Sandy Woodward was deeply concerned by the Argentinian radar capability. The Argentine GADA 601 AN/TPS-44 Mk II had a search range of 400km (248 miles); the AN/TPS-43 185km (114 miles) in the local climate. Able to pinpoint the Task Force at sea by tracking the path of Harriers returning to Woodward's carriers, it posed a great operational threat to his task force at sea and ultimately to Operation *Sutton*, and it increased the threat posed by Mirage fighters and Super Étendard strike aircraft armed with Exocet missiles.

Vulcans XM607, XM612, XM597 and XL391 were fitted with a Waddington-manufactured weapons pylon for the AS.37 Martel bolted under their port wings. Trials with weapons were conducted and training missions flown by all four Vulcans. Despite the mishap at the range in Wales, the Martel option was still on, as an early trial of the AGM-45A-10 did not work due to avionics problems. Authority to strike the radar sites using the Martel was given, to steel the frayed nerves aboard the Task Force.

Before the hunting started, four Martel technicians led by Sergeant Clive Atkey arrived at Wideawake from RAF Marham at 0500hrs on 13 May in preparation for the Martel-equipped Vulcans' arrival. Wing Commander John Morgan (the Officer Commanding Engineering) and Jerry Price queried whether the Martel team were also capable of arming the iron bombs; Mel James confirmed

Built at Puerto Belgrano by Captain Navio Pérez, this is an improvised manufactured unit: a double land-based launcher with M38 Exocet anti-ship missiles on a trailer with a separate power generator from a German 1938 searchlight unit. The M38 missiles were from the corvette *Guerrico* (P32). It was transferred on 31 May to the Malvinas in two Hercules C-130s. Four Exocet missiles were used between 1 and 12 June. One misfired on the launch; another mistakenly hit a bank; the third hit the destroyer HMS *Glamorgan* (D-19). The fourth missile was not fired. (Photo by Terence Laheney/Getty Images)

that they were not, so an armourer based at Coltishall, who was a BL755 cluster munitions expert, was flown out on board a VC-10 from Brize Norton, as Northwood might authorize Vulcans to carry BL755s. Air Commander Sir John Curtiss was keeping his options open.

In Washington DC, Air Vice Marshal Ron Dick was 18 months into his role as the British Air Attaché; he had also worked on the staff at Supreme Headquarters Allied Powers Europe (SHAPE) under Alexander Haig, now the US Secretary of State, when Haig had been the general commanding NATO forces in Europe. At a Washington reception, a director of Westinghouse sought out Air Vice Marshal Dick, and discreetly offered specifications and technical drawings on their radar. The air vice-marshal thought that the idea of receiving this information was unwise, pushing the boundaries of ethical behaviour. The director disagreed, pointing out that if the RAF could destroy the radar, Westinghouse would be able to sell the Argentinians a replacement!

Tubes with technical drawings duly arrived marked 'Urgent' and were dispatched as priority to England in the diplomatic bag. As a result, the British requested through Washington permission to access and use the American stockpile of AGM-45A-10 Shrike anti-radar missiles. This 'Dash 10' variant looked at the part of the spectrum where the AN/TPS-43 early warning radar resided. In contrast, the AGM-45A-9 'Dash 9' variant would specifically search for the Skyguard and Superfledermaus radars that supported the anti-aircraft guns.

Early in the pre-dawn of 15 May, an American cargo aircraft arrived on Ascension with a shipment for Bryden. The pallets, weighing 36,100lb, contained the first of an order for 300 AIM–9L Sidewinder missiles ordered on 13 May by John Nott. These 100 Sidewinders were transferred to Captain Bob McQueen. The resources of Pan Am were again in use on the apron as Martin Withers touched down at 0448hrs in XM607 to join XM612, armed with Martel and an updated ECM pod for the rescheduled *Black Buck 3* mission.

Vulcan XM607 was squeezed onto an already crammed apron for technical checks. There were problems on XM607, including issues with the weapons release sensor, the probe leak inside the radome, the intercom and the No.1 port tank (which was under-reading by 400lb). In addition, the Carousel navigation system was unserviceable. Work on XM612 revealed a precarious fuel state, leading to the question of whether a fuel tank had partially collapsed and therefore that the aircraft could not be properly refuelled by MAN fuel bowser. An analysis of total content (fuel bowser 18,975lb, XM612 dial indicating 17,900lb) showed that the aircraft was under-reading by about 1,000lb. A full check began, whereupon the total content was indicated as 73,800lb, while in reality there was nearer 74,800lb. There was also a slight discrepancy on the starboard group of fuel tanks, which was resolved. The work that it took to keep the Vulcans capable of extreme missions such as *Black Buck* was considerable.

The A-4Q Skyhawk built in 1972 (145050) became part of 3.ª Escuadrilla Aeronaval de Caza y Ataque. 3-A-214 (s.0667) was piloted by Frigate Lieutenant Marquez. On 21 May 1982, Marquez was intercepted by Lieutenant John Leeming near San Carlos. Sidewinders malfunctioned on Leeming's Sea Harrier so he switched to 'guns' and, at 150yds, fired a 30mm cannon that struck home just behind the cockpit. The A-4Q Skyhawk exploded. (Photo by Luis Rosendo/Heritage Images via Getty Images)

By the afternoon tension was ramped up in preparation for the rescheduled *Black Buck 3*. Technicians carried out functionals, and XM607 and XM612 were readied. However, at 1900hrs Mel James spoke with Jerry Price and Air Staff Operations Air Marshal Kenneth Hayr. The technicians were ordered to remove the Martel pylons immediately, which took one and a quarter hours. Technicians covered pylon holes in wings with speed tape, an aluminium pressure-sensitive tape used to perform minor repairs. At 2200hrs the Vulcans were positioned back by the all-white wooden 'Nose Hangar', a remnant of World War Two.

Despite the removal of the Martel systems, the crews hoped that *Black Buck 3* could finally be flown. However, on 17 May, Wideawake was trialling the installation of

Harpoon missiles on two Nimrods, with the assistance of US Navy personnel.[10] The Vulcans stayed on the ground, and *Black Buck 3* would not be flown.

On 18 May another abortive *Black Buck* raid was launched. Shortly before 1045hrs Montgomery took off from Wideawake in XM612. During the first air-to-air refuelling bracket, Montgomery edged the Vulcan's refuelling probe towards the Victor's basket. As always, the crew was relieved to hear the clunk from the safe contact, and fuel streamed through the hose. But there was damage: the Vulcan took on 10,000lb of fuel but its probe was distorted: rivets had sheared on the nozzle, but remained attached on XM612. The connection was broken, and a frustrated Montgomery was forced to return to Ascension. On the apron further faults were found: a canopy leak, and two door seals required replacements. The probe was changed but fuel flooded the radome; the inner pipe was distorted and a new one required, which was fitted on 23 May when the aircraft returned to Waddington. At 0815hrs on 20 May, Montgomery departed in XM607 for Waddington.[11] Martin Withers and his crew, with Squadron Leader Neil McDougall, Squadron Leader William Sherlock and Flight Lieutenant George Turfrey of Waddington's Operations Centre team, returned on a VC-10 to Britain.

Enter the Shrike

At Waddington, by 19 May a supply of AGM-45A Shrike missiles, as well as components for aircrew and engineer training, had been established.[12] USAF F-4G 'Wild Weasel' Phantoms, the specialist radar-hunting users of the AGM-45A, also touched down from Spangdahlem Air Force Base in West Germany to support the aircrew integration. Additionally, technicians arrived from Naval Air Station China Lake, Nevada, where the Shrike had been developed in 1963, to assist the meshing together. A single missile was initially attached to XM597 using a custom-made suspension pylon fabricated by RAF St Athan technicians in Wales, as none had ever existed. It was configured to accommodate one Shrike under each wing, utilizing the former Skybolt/Martel weapons point with wiring looms and internal instrumentation fitted, and a trial was performed. Then an American twin-launcher was rapidly adapted for the Vulcan to carry a pair of AGM-45A Shrikes under each wing. It worked, and the Shrike modification had gone from concept to mission-ready in just ten days. A timeline at the Ministry of Defence at Boscombe Down to fit Shrike on a Vulcan would have been a four-year project.

On Ascension at 0145hrs on 24 May, the first signal was received for a potential deployment of Vulcans for a *Black Buck* mission on 25 May at 1500Z. This was then aborted

10 Secretary Weinberger had recently approved eight Harpoon anti-ship missiles to the UK/Ascension with the transfer of information and equipment to assess the feasibility of converting Nimrod aircraft into Harpoon platforms. This was followed by the delivery of 20–34 Harpoon missiles and the equipment to perform Nimrod conversions in the UK.

11 Vulcan XM612 returned to Waddington on Sunday, 23 May 1982.

12 Officially 19 May 1982 is given as the date when AGM-45A Shrike arrived; however within the Ronald Reagan Library 280, a memorandum dated 20 May 1982, in response to President Reagan's Query on 18 May 'Regarding Vulcan OPS', states that 'last week' both Vulcans (XM597 and XM598) were returned to Waddington for refit to accommodate SHRIKE anti-radiation missiles, noting that 'on 18 May refit did not work Avionic problems so Vulcans equipped for MARTEL missiles instead for Ops.'

and rescheduled, and the RAF ordered Vulcans XM597 and XM598 with their new Shrike missiles to Ascension on 27 May. With insufficient time to test the system further, Neil McDougall flew XM598 out, testing the electronics on the way by getting a missile lock on the air traffic control at St Mawgan, Cornwall. It somewhat rankled with St Mawgan base commander Tony Woodford, an RAF officer outside the Operation *Corporate* chain of command, that there was no prior notice given.

That day a C-141 Starlifter arrived with further US technical backup at Wideawake. The second Vulcan crew, that of XM597, was more fortunate, as missiles could be test-fired before they were deployed to Ascension Island on the same day. Both Vulcans were then rearmed with AGM-45A missiles on Wideawake; XM597 and XM598 now carried an additional 16,000lb of fuel in bomb-bay tanks which extended their range and reduced the number of refuelling contacts needed on the flight to the Falklands to four Victor K2s.

Landing at San Carlos

Under the codename Operation *Sutton*, the British landed at its beachhead in San Carlos Water, 65 miles away from Stanley on 21 May.[13] With the Argentine surface fleet remaining in port after the sinking of *Belgrano* and the blockade around the Falklands continuing, the task to oppose the landings fell to the pilots of Argentine Air Force and Argentine Naval Aviation. At 500 miles – about 50 minutes' flying time – from mainland south America, their Daggers, Mirages and Skyhawks were at the limit of their fuel tank range, and so had only seconds to release their bombs before heading home again. At 1015hrs the first wave arrived. The second at 1337hrs, leaving HMS *Argonaut* without power. At 1800hrs, Skyhawks hit HMS *Ardent*. Suffering devastating damage, the ship sank on 22 May. On the 23rd, Skyhawks scythed through the air to catch HMS *Antelope* which sank. British troop transports RFA *Sir Lancelot*, *Sir Galahad*[14] and *Sir Bedivere* were attacked by Skyhawks and Daggers, along with the heavily laden ammunition ship *Resource*, anchored in San Carlos Water. All survived after the Argentines got their time-fuses wrong.[15] Then, on 25 May, HMS *Coventry* was overwhelmed by wave after wave of Skyhawks until it was abandoned and sank. However, the Argentine Naval Aviation arm was not finished for the day.

GADA radar operators on the Falklands identified a possible target 176km to the northeast. Two Super Étendard armed with Exocets were scrambled from Río Grande. After being refuelled by KC-130 Tanker, weaving inches above the ocean, Corvette Captain Roberto Curilovic and Lieutenant Julio Barraza located the target exactly where the radar had predicted. Coordinates were loaded into their weapons' systems and they launched the Exocets at 1831hrs and turned back. The French-built missiles passed the chaff countermeasure dispensed by HMS *Ambuscade* twenty-four miles from their target, adjusted streaking over the water for another four miles then crashed through SS *Atlantic Conveyor*'s port quarter – nine feet above the waterline with an enormous explosion. *Conveyor* was a total loss.

13   President's national security briefing, attended by George Bush, William Clark and Robert McFarlane and held in the Oval Office from 1010 hours until 1025 hours on 18 May (Reagan Library, President's Daily Diary); the plan was to have VULCAN sorties soften up/disrupt Argentine C3 (command, control and communications systems) concurrent with landing in San Carlos.

14   Royal Fleet Auxiliary landing ship *Sir Galahad*, destroyed by bombs on June 8 with the loss of 48 lives; another landing ship sustained damage.

15   Argentine MK–82 bombs struck six ships and did not explode: fuses may have been defective (19 July 1982: Military Lessons from the Falklands).

With these setbacks and losses, it was imperative the RAF acted. Admiral Sandy Woodward wanted the Argentine radar systems eliminated. In New York Jeane Kirkpatrick, United States Ambassador to the United Nations, and a strong supporter of Argentina, met with Argentinian Air Force General Jose Miret, and with Alberto Manen, the Air Attaché's aide to Argentina's Embassy in Washington. Miret was skeptical that the British San Carlos beachhead would hold as Argentine aircraft had inflicted severe damage and sunk naval ships. Although the military situation favoured Argentina having coordinated attacks using land-based radar with their aircraft, Argentinian commanders were aware that ultimately Britain would expand the war zone by using 'smart weapons' against land-based targets.

A Grumman S-2A Tracker 2-AS-21 on the *Veinticinco de Mayo*, the aircraft carrier wearing the typical grey/white colour scheme of the US Navy. The airframe was acquired by *Comando de la Aviación Naval Argentina* (Argentine Naval Aviation Command) in 1962. In the Falklands War, 2-AS-21 flew anti-submarine and search and rescue missions. (Photo by Luis Rosendo/Heritage Images via Getty Images)

On Friday 28 May, *Black Buck 4*, the first planned 'Shrike' anti-radiation missile strike, was green lighted. The fuel plan called for six Victor K2 Tankers supporting one Vulcan flown by Squadron Leader Neil McDougall, although an airborne spare Victor and Vulcan would launch with the outbound wave to cover 'unserviceabilities' once in the air. In the end seven tankers launched at 1-minute intervals at 00:00Z, followed by a slightly delayed extra K2 flown by Andy Tomalin at 0017hrs. Once airborne, Tomalin's aircraft suffered a Hose Drum Unit failure and returned to Ascension. The sortie proceeded as far as the fourth refuelling area, or Bracket 4 some 1790nm south of Ascension. Bob Tuxford was flying one of the two short slots, which involved giving a single large transfer of fuel to a Victor tanker 500nm or so south of Ascension, and a second transfer to two of the other tankers in the formation, resulting in Tuxford and Elliott returning after a little over two and a half hours in the air. The remaining three Victors continued with the Vulcan via the 2nd and 3rd air-to-air refuelling brackets, to the 4th bracket. This entailed two of the Victors mutually refuelling, whilst the third refuelled the Vulcan for the second time. At some point during these transfers, roughly four hours into the task, one of the tankers suffered a Hose Drum Unit malfunction which could only result in the mission being aborted. The loss of one tanker out of three at this point could not be tolerated from a point of view of remaining fuel within the serviceable tankers. Relaying their predicament to Ops, Tanker Ops on Wideawake had no alternative but to confirm that the mission would have to be aborted. Recall of the recovery wave followed, which involved the inbound wave of a further three Victor K2s which had, by this time, launched before the failure incident. Tomalin having dropped out of the outbound wave, was used a second time that night in another aircraft, and as a result, was recalled from his second abortive sortie that night. The mission would be rescheduled to go ahead the next day. Curtiss conveyed this by satellite phone to Woodward, who was extremely frustrated that the air campaign against Argentine radar had not got off to a good start. 'Beginning to wonder how these people are earning their keep,' noted Sandy Woodward.[16]

Repairing and relocating the radars

Following the Sea Harrier and Vulcan strikes on the island's airport, Argentinian defensive weapon systems required more than the usual maintenance. One of GADA 602's Roland SAM generators malfunctioned, but luckily Manfred Jentges, a technician from the Franco-German manufacturer Euromissile arrived. Jentges had been in Mar del Plata, Argentina,

Argentine radar technicians begin camouflaging their position between the homes and outbuildings of Davis Street, Dairy Paddock Road and Brisbane Road in Stanley. (Carlos Mazzoch)

on vacation with another two French technicians. Jentges fixed the platelet in the generator while other components were repaired at the Balseiro Institute in the Andes. Other faults identified by First Lieutenant Carlos Regalini's GADA 602 men were resolved before checking a Westinghouse AN/TPS-43, then GADA 601's AN/TPS-44, and Rheinmetall fire-control radar. The newly repaired components were fitted and the Roland SAM was fully operational at 1800hrs on 18 May. Manfred Jentges then hitched a ride on a C-130 back to Argentina.

Commander Miguel Silva of GADA 601 was ordered to disassemble his AN/TPS-44 and move location, to reassemble then camouflage the vital site. Silva situated the radar in a smallholding bisected by Dairy Paddock Road, Davis Street and Brisbane Road in Stanley. The outhouse height contour was similar to the height of the antenna. The technicians' cabin was sited nearby. Both were shielded from the seaward side, with the antenna occasionally visible during its 360-degree sweeps at six revolutions per minute. Using cable extensions, Lieutenant Guillermo Saravia was able to position the fire-control unit 229ft away halfway between the two generators and the jerrycans. The operators' cabins were fortified using 18 discarded 200-litre steel drums filled with peat, with a top layer of corrugated metal sheets fortified with sandbags. Sky-blue paint blended the drums in with the neat picket fences and wooden verandas, as ducks and chickens ran around.

In the event of an attack, the radio frequency emission had to be manually cut off by a radar mechanic dashing from the operational cabin to the technical cabin near the antenna, who would then 'cut high' (switch off the emissions). 'So he only had to fall or trip over, and there was a real risk of being hit,' said Lieutenant Carlos Mazzochi. A remote system was rigged up so that without moving from their cabin the operators could not only 'cut high' but could make the radar transmit again as well as stop the antenna's rotation so that it could be less easily spotted. Both radar technicians' and operators' training had taken place at the radar base in Merlo, near Buenos Aires, and at Patagonia. All were highly skilled, having operated on missions along the Argentinian border, and they had come up with an ingenious self-defence set-up.

Black Buck 5

Black Buck 5 was launched on 30 May in pitch-black skies. Four Victor tankers dragging long hoses illuminated by their navigation lights fed XM597 fuel. After refuelling, the lights were extinguished: Vulcan XM597 was off to war on its own. Early in the pre-dawn of 31 May, AN/TPS-43F operators detected shipping and aircraft from 0416hrs through to 0544hrs, when precision attacks by Sea Harriers hit the airport. This meant that the commanders in BAM Malvinas' (Stanley's) command centre called for the AN/TPS-43F to be kept online to help with defence. Ensign Alf Mercau had a continuous threat up to 186 miles on his console, which was initially thought to be a Sea Harrier, but was actually XM597 piloted by Neil McDougall and armed with two AGM-45 Shrikes. After 12 miles, the echo disappeared. Mercau grabbed the 'cut high', switching off the power and forcing the Vulcan to restart the process.

XM597 had descended to 300ft when approximately 200 miles from the Falklands. At 20 miles the V-bomber climbed to 16,000ft and air electronics officer Rod Trevaskus scanned for AN/TPS-43 emissions; then McDougall changed to headings indicated on Trevaskus' console with azimuth and elevation bars. After orbiting for almost an hour, on the ground,

Mercau had been forced to turn on the radar. In the last of their turns, Trevaskus picked up signals from their primary target, and the range-critical Shrike missiles were launched. As a first-generation anti-radiation missile, the Shrike was unable to 'remember' the location of a radar which was switched off, so would be unlikely to hit the target.

One landed 32ft away from the AN/TPS-43F antenna and the second hit an abandoned house. One of their two trucks took the full force of the blast, two pieces of shrapnel slicing the waveguide that transferred the communication signals, resulting in the radar becoming unserviceable. Another piece severed the communications cable linking the technicians' and operators' cabins. The two explosions unleashed a volley of shock waves; water pipes burst, walls crumbled and windows were blown out while the radar technicians' and operators' hearing was impaired from the secondary wave and they were left gasping for air. First Lieutenant Faber, Ensign Alf Mercau, First Corporal Egañas, Principal Corporal Rosset, Principal Corporal Barrios and First Corporal Ulrich stood up and checked themselves over; none had any major injuries. After making an assessment Miguel Silva signalled for replacement parts. A LADA C-130 brought them in and within 39 hours, by 2100hrs on Tuesday 1 June, the radar was fully functional. 'Our manual countermeasures had worked and saved lives,' one veteran wrote.

Black Buck 6

On 2 June, Wing Commander Peter Squires of No. 1 (F) Squadron with Flight Lieutenant Edward Balls of 800 NAS as wingman flew a night mission between Bluff Cove and Goose Green, with Squires strafing a suspected Argentine mobile Israeli ELTA radar at Mount Usborne. As both turned back to *Hermes* to land, dauntingly stiff headwinds and sea fog encroached. Weather thus impacted operations, forcing changes in combat planning. With Sea Harriers and Harrier GR.3s grounded on 3 June, there would be no decoy mission for *Black Buck 6*.

Minor faults kept Vulcans XM597 and XM598 on the ground at Wideawake before *Black Buck 6* commenced. Lessons learned during the previous *Black Buck 5* showed that XM597 had been momentarily locked onto by a Contraves Skyguard. On 3 June, the Vulcans switched to using one pair of Dash-10 and one pair of Dash-9 Shrikes. However, the RAF lacked adequate intelligence to identify the new GADA radar sites. McDougall flew the primary Vulcan, XM597. He flew blind, reliant on Rod Trevaskus and Flight Lieutenant Dave Castle (Nav Radar) to plot either location.

On the islands, First Lieutenant Alejandro Dachary received his orders to shift position too. The 601 GADA Skyguard was directed to the outskirts of Stanley on 2 June. At the AN/TPS-43 site Miguel Silva was in charge of the shift from 0500hrs local time on 3 June; at 0650hrs his radar controllers detected raiders on the same track as the previous ones, this time detecting them at 186 miles on the azimuth 030 degrees with a speed of 250kt.

Vulcan B.2/*Black Buck 5* targets a Westinghouse AN/TPS-43 3D radar, 31 May 1982

On 31 May 1982, Avro Vulcan XM597 was deployed carrying a pair of AGM-45 Shrike anti-radiation missiles with a DASH-10 ECM. Squadron Leader, Neil McDougall, piloting XM597, kept off whilst a Sea Harriers attack was staged on Port Stanley airport designed to coincide with the attack from the Vulcan to force the defenders to turn on their radar. Vulcan XM597 twisted and turned before the crew got a lock-on and were able to launch the missiles. At 0845Z, two Shrikes were launched. One of them fell about 8 to 10m from the antenna, but most of its shrapnel was absorbed by the 601 GADA truck positioned between the impact area and the antenna. This illustration shows Vulcan XM597 flying through cloud cover with two of its launched Shrike missiles hurtling towards their target.

The Vulcan disappeared after five rotations of the antenna (around 50 seconds), and was then seen to descend to low level, reappearing at 34 miles on the azimuth 330 degrees. Immediately the controllers switched off when XM597 was 16 miles out from Stanley. This started a game of 'hide and seek', whereby the controllers searched for and located both the Vulcan and other flights, and would then automatically (completely) shut down every time the Vulcan faced directly onto their radar.

By now, McDougall had been pirouetting in the sky above Stanley for an hour. 'We've enough fuel for one more circuit,' said co-pilot Flying Officer Chris Lackman. Then came a breakthrough. Rod Trevaskus heard a sound in his headset from a Skyguard and asked Dave Castle to ascertain the location. 'Looks like a Skyguard emitter close to the airfield,' he said into the intercom. 'I've got my markers over its possible location. We could prosecute an attack if we've enough fuel.'

Lackman acknowledged that they had ten minutes. The reaction that McDougall, Trevaskus and Castle were looking for came when McDougall swung XM597 northwards. His next manoeuvre was gut-wrenching as the nose was tipped forward into a vertical dive. 'Ten thousand feet,' exclaimed Flight Lieutenant Barry Smith (Nav Plotter), then suddenly the Shrike consul lit up – a faint signal. Their rapid descent had enticed GADA 601's Skyguard to lock onto the Vulcan. With a slight adjustment two Shrikes locked on; Trevaskus pressed the fire button and off they went. The radio altimeter registered 7,000ft, then 6,000ft. A split-second later XM597 encountered a firestorm of accurate radar-directed Oerlikon 35mm flak; 550 rounds per minute were being pumped out, but fortunately all exploded below the Vulcan. Neil McDougall instinctively took evasive action, hauling the V-bomber to 13,000ft. At his console Smith counted down the time of impact.

On the ground conscript Ariel Tascon came off duty, and stepped out of the Skyguard cabin to hear jet engines somewhere in the grey sky. Unsure whether they were Argentinian or British, he entered one of buildings to chat with the woman who rented the homestead out to GADA 601.

The Skyguard team had also tracked the plane heading towards Stanley, Dachary receiving orders to keep the system operational. He had reduced their pulse emissions to the minimum to enable to operate all their defensive firepower. At roughly 0620hrs, the Skyguard alarm shrilled that all power was cut, which also disabled their gun-laying control to the Oerlikons. Then a Shrike warhead exploded. There was a loud whumph! The ground shuddered; in its wake the cabin caught a cascade of shrapnel, shredding electronics and people. Four were killed. First Lieutenant Alejandro Dachary, Sergeant René Blanco, conscript's Oscar Diarte,

Outside of the GADA 601 Skyguard cabin that at 0620hrs caught the blast from the Shrike missile fired by XM597. The explosion killed First Lieutenant Alejandro Dachary, Sergeant René Blanco, S/C Oscar Diarte, and S/C José Llamas. (Andrew D. Bird Collection)

and José Llamas were sitting in their seats within the cabin's confined space amongst the smouldering electrical fire as rescuers looked for signs of life while choking smoke stung their eyes, noses and throats. There were no respirators or breathing apparatus available but rescuers persevered, hauling out one survivor as others watched and waited. Outside, Tascon had had a harrowingly close call. Everyone that day was really frightened, despite denials.

An hour after the missile strike an order was received from BAM Malvinas headquarters to avoid leaving any Skyguard on permanently. The crisis caused a quarrel with senior officers as the threat posed by the radar blackout reduced Argentine air defence capabilities on the islands and the mainland-based fighters lost their radar-dependent capability to intercept. Major Hugo Maiorano subsequently told senior officers enquiring into the radar blackout that they should have heeded the warnings of the commanders – Dachary and Lieutenant Oscar Spath – that their radar signature could be seen and increased their vulnerability if left on.

An unscheduled stopover

Neil McDougall had accomplished the task of steering XM597 the 3,955 miles to the target, and now had to guide the Vulcan a further 2,236 miles to close in on Bracket One, initiating pre-refuelling checks. Next to him the air-to-air refuelling instructor, Flight Lieutenant Brian Gardner, kept an eye on McDougall as he nosed the aircraft towards Victor XH673 flown by Flight Lieutenant Andy Barrett.

The 90-ton delta-winged bomber's refuelling probe approached XH673's basket eight times with four brushes of the basket rim. Gardner suggested that the fatigued Neil McDougall swap out with Chris Lackman as he, Gardner, wasn't allowed in the right-hand seat. Refusing, McDougall approached for another attempt. Gardner watched with mounting alarm.

Bumping the rim again, with too much force exerted, the valve from the probe broke off as it was designed to, allowing McDougall to exit. He instinctively broke off the contact, and fuel poured over the aircraft. Amber lights followed, necessitating an emergency diversion to Río de Janeiro, Brazil. With a muttered expletive over the intercom Neil McDougall steadied XM597, buffeted by the backwash. 'An understatement if ever I heard one,' came a voice through headphones.

Chris Lackman did the arithmetic: their tanks held 13,500lb of fuel. Dave Castle and Barry Smith searched for charts; everything for such an emergency had been plundered by Victor and Nimrod aircrews, such were the scant logistical resources available to RAF crews. The pair produced a poor photocopy of radio frequencies for Brazilian airspace.

However, their situation got more alarming. The needles of their fuel gauges were plummeting rapidly, as a fractured fuel pipe was leaking liquid between wing tanks and their bomb bay fuel tank. There was little chance of reaching the Brazilian coast if McDougall kept the aircraft at the refuelling height, so he climbed to 40,000ft to conserve the remaining fuel. Lackman tried desperately to find a fix but more fuel was drained in the process. Castle adjusted his radar markers to Río de Janeiro and gave co-ordinates to steer. Trevaskus queried how they were going to explain their situation to the Brazilian authorities. Then Smith enquired about their two remaining Shrike missiles slung under their port wing. McDougall suggested they jettison them.

There was a slight problem: technicians had not managed to fit a safe-jettison wiring system, so the only option was to live-fire the missiles. Castle switched on their HS2, checking for any surface ships. Fifty miles ahead was a large fishing fleet on a westerly bearing so McDougall turned XM597 through 90 degrees onto a southerly heading for Trevaskus to fire the pair of missiles. One left the pylon but the second malfunctioned, and despite repeatedly pressing the firing button the Shrike wouldn't budge.

McDougall and Gardner brought the Vulcan back on to a westerly course when another problem popped up: they had on board quantities of sensitive and classified material that would be

Vulcan XM597 crew (left to right): navigation plotter Barry Smith; air electronics officer Rod Trevaskus; co-pilot Chris Lackman; third pilot Brian Gardner, radar navigator David Castle; captain Neil McDougall; Wing Commander Jeremy 'Jerry' Brown, Air Attaché; and commander of Galeão Air Force Base Cel Av José Teófilo Rodrigues de Aquino with his wife and family. (Moraes Filho, Brazilian Air Force)

EVENTS

1. 0650hrs. At Port Stanley, the Argentine 601 GADA Skyguard air-defence radar detects an aircraft 186 miles away.

2. At 34 miles out, Vulcan XM597 descends.

3. Argentine radar controllers switch off AN/TPS-43 when the Vulcan is 16 miles from Stanley airport.

4. Fifty miles to entry point, Vulcan XM597 switches on ECM and H2S at 12,000ft.

5. Vulcan XM597 makes first loop over Falkland Islands at height of 12,000ft.

6. Vulcan XM597 makes second loop over Falkland Islands.

7. Vulcan XM597 reduces height from 12,000ft on a new flightpath; Argentinian radar contact kicks in at 10,000ft.

8. On a third flightpath, Argentinian radar contact is made at 18 miles at 10,000ft.

9. For ten miles, the pilot decreases his height to 6,000ft. Two Shrike missiles lock onto their target at Stanley airport.

10. Argentine 601 GADA Skyguard defence makes contact at 6,000ft, six miles out and opens fire. AAA shells explode approximately 1,000ft below the Vulcan, which climbs to 13,000ft and exits.

11. 0620hrs. Skyguard power is switched off; 25 seconds later, two Shrike missiles explode.

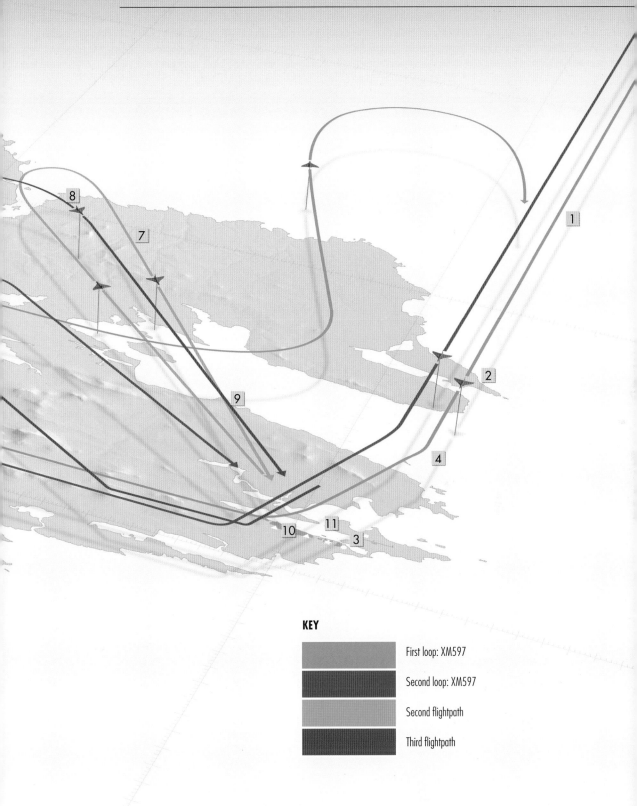

KEY

First loop: XM597

Second loop: XM597

Second flightpath

Third flightpath

potentially an intelligence windfall for the Brazilian authorities. That meant opening the escape hatch and chucking the lot out. If only it were that simple.

It meant depressurizing the aircraft cabin, then opening the escape hatch in flight at 43,000ft. With their oxygen masks tightly fitted with goggles down, and their masks on 100 per cent oxygen, the Vulcan commenced depressurizing. There was a pop, then a mist in the cockpit as water droplets condensed then cooled under pressure. The fall in pressure saw their regulators force-feed 100 per cent oxygen into their masks. Suddenly breathing and talking became an effort.

The mist dispersed and everyone was reassuringly okay. Then the silence was broken by Barry Smith flicking the Bakelite switch positioned underneath his table to open the escape hatch door (also used to access the aircraft in normal circumstances), which automatically opened outwards, using hydraulic jacks. In seconds there was a deafening high-pitched noise, then as if on cue, Brian Gardner arrived with the aircrew aluminium ration box crammed with material weighted down by an undercarriage lock; both Castle and Gardner then precariously shoved and prodded the ration box to the lip of the hatch for it to fall away.

Unfortunately, the hatch now wouldn't close. Gardner pressed the switch, but a fail-safe mechanism meant that the hatch locked automatically when opened, and could now only be unlocked and closed manually. However, to reach the door handle to disengage it from the locked position Castle had to use the crew ladder which had been left on Ascension. Castle's exasperated expression said it all. With Castle's arms clenched around Gardner's waist the pair stepped towards the hatch. To hang out into a 300kt airstream Gardner straddled the hatch then stretched his right arm out to grasp the handle. With hand gestures Castle adjusted his grip to Gardner's lower torso. Success, but the handle was firmly fixed in the locked position. An escape knife from Castle gave Gardner the leverage to force the mechanism into the unlocked position then slam it shut. While the frenetic activity to close the escape hatch had been going on, air electronics officer Rod Trevaskus had turned the radio to VHF 121.5, the emergency frequency for civilian aircraft as opposed to military air distress, on 243.0 MHz. 'Mayday, Mayday, Mayday! This is Ascot Five Nine Seven. We are a commercial flight. We have an emergency. We are short on fuel.'

The Río Sector controller requested their call sign again, country of departure and destination. Through either ignorance or arrogance, none of the RAF aviators on board realized that their bomber was being tracked by Brazil's Integrated Center for Air Defense and Air Traffic Control in Brasília, and that Brazil was fully aware that this was a military flight. Brazilian military officers followed the communication between the Río Sector controller and RAF jet bomber, waiting in silence for the identification of the aircraft that presented itself as a civil aircraft. 'Their lampooning brought an atmosphere of distrust for our defence operators,' recalled Major José Orlando Bellon of the Military Operations Center.

During a pause in communication the Vulcan was re-pressurized. Flight Lieutenant Nigel Rough, piloting Nimrod XV227 and Flight Lieutenant Andy Barrett's XH673 were both in a holding pattern on the edge of Brazilian airspace. Wing Commander David Emmerson on board XV227 as navigator realized that the situation had become increasingly tense and was potentially explosive. Rough's operators relayed information on the unfolding crisis to Northwood but it proved difficult using only a single-sideband HF radio so messages were sent via Ascension back to Britain. Emmerson gave advice to McDougall before breaking off when Rough and Barrett headed for Wideawake.

With 'The A-Team' etched in red onto the left side of Victor XH673, Andy Barrett's crew on *Black Buck 6*. Left to right: navigator radar Ash Holmes; captain Andy Barrett; air electronics officer Patrick 'Taff' Bland; navigator plotter John Hendy; co-pilot Tony Ingelbrecht. (Brian Armstrong)

There was a considerable rise in confidence, buoyed even more when the Brasília Sector controllers accepted them for landing. Rod Trevaskus noticed that the person's voice had changed after they mentioned Huddersfield as their point of departure. Their aircraft automatically passed to Bellon's Brazilian Air Force fighter controllers. 'No doubt they were enjoying the hilarity enormously,' Bellon said. After conferring with officers, the fighter controller activated *1º Grupo de Aviação de Caça* (1st Fighter Aviation Group). At 1050hrs local time their alert siren sounded at Santa Cruz air base.

Northrop F-5E Tiger IIs of 2º Esquadrão, part of the 1º Grupo de Aviação de Caça, based at Santa Cruz Air Base, in June 1982. (Moraes Filho, Brazilian Air Force)

The alert fighters had been scrambled on another job. Captains Raul José Ferreira Dias and Marco Aurélio dos Santos Coelho had just finished their external checks on their *2º Esquadrão* (2nd Squadron) Northrop F-5E Tigers. Dias and Coelho's original mission was an exercise of low-level navigation with reconnaissance photography. In seconds their status changed to Quick Reaction Alert fighters. Armourers appeared with drums of 20mm cannon and trollies with four AIM-9 Sidewinder missiles. Raul Dias talked with the technician pulling his ladder away, who suggested he plug his communication leads in. He then heard in his headset Operational Fighter Control making desperate pleas, using the words 'Rojão de Fogo' – meaning this is a real-time live mission not a simulation. Both jets slipped seamlessly along the runway into the air. Dias and Coelho heard 'Supersônico' over Guanabara Bay; their sonic booms were heard on the ground, causing mild panic as the fighter jets climbed quickly.

Instructions were passed to Raul Dias. Initially three aircraft were identified (a Nimrod, Victor and Vulcan); however, in seconds this changed as two departed (the Nimrod and the Victor) and were no longer perceived as a threat. Their controller gave Dias the correct bearing and flight level to intercept the Vulcan 185 miles south of Río.

'We've a visual,' said Dias, 'Weapons system live.'

They approached the distinctive shape of the British 1950s delta-wing Vulcan bomber, then separated to go either side slightly aft. Dias switched radio frequency to the civilian aircraft emergency frequency VHF 121.5 but McDougall did not reply. Dias got no response a second time either. Marco Coelho positioned his fighter astern as Raul Dias edged his F-5E closer on the starboard side at the same altitude as XM597 and got a response.

Trevaskus heard instructions to divert to Santa Cruz air base, but with fuel tanks virtually dry Neil McDougall refused. Raul Dias noticed that the refuelling probe on the nose was broken. Controllers guided the trio through 21 in-flight commercial jet airliners during their descent to 16,000ft, crossing the Brazilian coast. They then instructed Ascot 597 that the Vulcan was cleared to land at Galeão on runway One-Zero Two-Eight, the duty runway.

Vulcan B.2/*Black Buck 6* escorted into Rio, 3 June 1982

On 3 June 1982, Avro Vulcan XM597 successfully fired two AGM-45 Shrike anti-radiation missiles. Squadron leader, Neil McDougall, piloting XM597, was, however, forced to divert to Rio de Janeiro in Brazil during the return trip when its in-flight refuelling probe broke. After disposing of classified documents, on nearing the Brazilian air space two Brazilian Air Force 2º Esquadrão Northrop F-5E Tigers armed with AIM-9 Sidewinders were scrambled to intercept. Sloppy radio protocol by the crew of Vulcan XM597 with military air traffic controllers saw Captain Raul José Ferreira Dias close on its starboard side, with Marco Aurélio dos Santos Coelho dead astern. After repeated radio contact was ignored, there was a request from XM597 to divert and land. Controllers guided the trio through twenty-one commercial flights as they descended, taking them past the Christ the Redeemer (*Cristo Redentor*) statue overlooking Rio de Janeiro. Both F-5E Tigers followed interception protocol and stayed close until Vulcan XM597 touched down at Galeão Base, in Rio de Janeiro, at 11.50am local time.

Vulcan XM597 on the ground at Río being inspected by Brazilian Air Force personnel. (Moraes Filho, Brazilian Air Force)

Vulcan XM597 on the ground at Río with its broken nose probe. The remaining Shrike missile on the port hardpoint is shrouded. (Moraes Filho, Brazilian Air Force)

That meant a downwind flight path over the city. It was risky and they could not afford a technical fault or an engine(s) to cut out over the residential area near the airport.

'Negative,' McDougall replied asking, 'Are your jet fighters necessary?'

Neil McDougall was unfamiliar with South American politics and didn't realize that Brazil was in its 20th year of being governed by a military dictatorship. But regardless of this, he should have known that fighters would escort the 'threat' until it landed in one piece. These procedures are standard and remain valid up to today.

Hearing 'negative,' the controller gave the okay to land on the reciprocal runway, downwind, rather than into a light, five to ten knot breeze.

'Ascot 597, they're following interception protocol, both will stay with you until you're down ....'

At 10,000ft they were too high. McDougall throttled back, extended the airbrake and bled the speed off. He produced an airshow performance, standing Vulcan XM597 on its port wingtip then hauling the aircraft into a tight two- or three-G turn with 65 degrees of bank, emerging on the glide slope a mile and a half from the threshold but still making 300kt. Pulling the nose well up, he slowed to 150kt, dropped the wheels, and delivered a perfect landing at 1150hrs local time. Dias and Coelho in their F-5Es came in fast over the bomber, then broke right to repeat the process, before diverting to Santa Cruz air base, both performing a barrel roll in unison. They had completed 2º Esquadrão's first 'live' mission with armed weapons.

Rod Trevaskus jumped out of the Vulcan to render the single Shrike missile safe before XM597 halted away from commercial airliners. Margins had been close as the aircraft's fuel gauges on all four engines were indicating empty. The crew were greeted by armed troops and the base commander, José Teófilo Rodrigues de Aquino, who escorted them to the Brazilian Air Force officers' mess.

Defence Minister John Nott was informed at 2341hrs and information passed to the US Embassy in London as a courtesy that 'the plane carried a single Shrike missile which couldn't be jettisoned before the Vulcan made an emergency landing at Río de Janeiro.'

The British Air Attaché in Brazil was Wing Commander Jeremy 'Jerry' Brown. Since the outbreak of the Falklands War, the Brazilian Air Force had been intercepting cargo flown out of Cuba – an effort which Brown applauded. Instructing McDougall to comply with Brazilian requests he then focused on negotiating the release of both the crew, held securely in the officers' mess, and the aircraft; but first the question of the Shrike missile had to be dealt with. Brown informed Washington that the missile was in a lethal state since the firing mechanism had been activated. The Ministry of Defence sent instructions by fax to the British Embassy on how to disarm the Shrike, which were couriered over to the base. Nott was hopeful that the Vulcan XM597 and its weapon could be recovered quickly and with little public notice. The Brazilian Air Force provided airmen with a mattress which was positioned underneath the Shrike as they perused the Texas Instruments weapon manual.[17] With rudimentary tools they successfully released the missile from its pylon, then placed it in secure storage. Brown informed the US Embassy of the security arrangements that were being provided.

General Galtieri sent a note to the Brazilians requesting the detention of XM597 and crew until the end of the Falklands War. This would seriously disrupt negotiations, and Washington

2° Esquadrão fighter pilots based at Santa Cruz air base. Captain Raul José Ferreira Dias is front row third from left (with tiger patterned bone dome) and Captain Marco Aurélio dos Santos Coelho back row stands second from left. The pair intercepted Vulcan XM597 and guided into Galeão Air Force Base. (Moraes Filho, Brazilian Air Force)

wanted to avoid any mention of the Shrike, particularly since the US manufacturer had supplied the missile to Britain after the start of the Falklands War. The US Embassy in Brazil was requested to maintain as low a profile as possible during the Shrike recovery, and to treat the issue as a bilateral matter to the greatest extent possible.

The US Secretary of State, Alexander Haig, was with President Ronald Reagan in Paris, and both were informed by secure phone line of the Vulcan's unscheduled stop in Río. Their conversation with the Department of Defence was lengthy. The two men were in the country for the Versailles Economic Summit and were kept informed. Margaret Thatcher spoke to President Reagan briefly, and there was encouragement that all would be quickly sorted as Brazilian and British diplomats continued negotiations for the release of both aircraft and crew. By Friday 4 June, the first deal was struck, involving the procurement of Westland Lynx helicopter spares for the Brazilian Navy, which had become the helicopter's first foreign operator in 1978. The Brazilian Foreign Ministry was encouraged by this but for understandable regional diplomatic and political reasons the Vulcan stayed at Galeão.

After seven days the British and Americans were optimistic about the possibilities for a negotiated release of Squadron Leader Neil McDougall, his aircrew and Vulcan XM597. On Wednesday 9 June, there was another breakthrough during late-night negotiations, with terms being agreed that satisfied the Brazilians. Very quickly British Ambassador George Harding received assurances that McDougall, Lackman, Gardner, Trevaskus, Smith and Castle would be released the following day. Fuel for Vulcan XM597's outbound flight to Ascension was diplomatically handled by Brown and Harding. The RAF Vulcan bomber departed just before Pope John Paul II made a scheduled refuelling stopover in Río Janeiro on 10 June, before travelling on to Argentina.

'The Brazilian government decided to release the British Vulcan, which was at the Río military air base, on receipt of a formal undertaking by the British government not to use this plane any more in the current hostilities with Argentina,' said Foreign Ministry spokesman Bernardo Pericas.

Neil McDougall and his crew touched down on Ascension on runway One-Four. After taxiing off the runway, he and his crew shut down the engines and systems, unstrapped and clambered down the ladder. McDougall had completed the first emergency of its kind on a mission in the South Atlantic, and it had underlined just how dangerous and difficult these

17 Department of State, Central Foreign Policy File, D850363–0040; Telegram 4931 from Brasilia, 'June 14 Shrike missile has been removed from the Vulcan by the Brazilians'.

operations were. The plan was now to retain the crew and continue missions albeit in a different airframe. With a new refuelling probe fitted, Vulcan XM597 departed Ascension for the flight back to Waddington. On arrival Anthony Wright greeted McDougall and his crew, then led them to the base's operations room. There was a cacophony of noise from their families – they had made it home. In the true fashion of British bureaucracy, bar bills from the Brazilian officers' mess arrived from the British Embassy in Brasilia at RAF Waddington days later.

Black Buck 7

With the construction of a Harrier Forward Operating base at Port San Carlos with refuelling facilities, up to four aircraft could be parked on the strip at any one time. It allowed Harriers to extend their effective mission times from ten minutes on the scene to nearly an hour. Operations had begun on 5 June. Two Harrier GR.3s were detached each day to provide quick reaction support for ground forces. On 10 June close support missions were flown in support of ground troops near Two Sisters as Royal Marines and 2nd Parachute Regiment engaged Argentine troops during the advance towards the capital Port Stanley. At 0637hrs the following morning, Saturday 12 June, HMS *Glamorgan* providing fire support for these troops was damaged by an Argentine land-based MM38 Exocet missile. This prompted Admiral Sandy Woodward to enquire about another Shrike mission utilizing an RAF Harrier, two of which had been configured to carry the weapon. However, Major General Jeremy Moore suggested ground troops could take them over during the advance. Both Woodward and Moore were also concerned by the elusive Pucarás. 'We didn't know whereabouts they'd be from one minute to the next,' wrote the Task Force commander. With a military victory near at hand there could be no miscalculation. Moore, using a satellite phone, spoke to Northwood requesting Vulcan bomber support on 12th, from Ascension Islands as insurance. Martin Withers, and his crew, which included Flight Lieutenant Peter Standing as his onboard air-to-air refuelling instructor instead of Dick Russell, took-off at 0850hrs on the seventh, and final *Black Buck* operation. This strike marked the Vulcans' and RAF's last – and likely to remain so – heavy bomber operation in the annals of the service's history.

After connecting with five Victor K.2 Tankers, Vulcan XM607 approached Stanley airport using the same route as *Black Buck 1* and released 21 1,000lb iron bombs over the target. One of them hit the east corner of the track and exploded [on the opposite side of the other two missions]. The rest airburst and caused superficial shrapnel damage to facilities. 'Most of the airburst bomb fragments damaged personnel,' wrote Miguel Silva of 601 GADA, 'and did not pierce the runway, since the war was ending and the airport was needed to deploy their Phantom fighters.'[18] Withers hauled Victor XM607 away from the airfield and headed nearly due north to a planned rendezvous with a Victor for the first inbound fuel bracket, eventually landing back at Ascension.

The post-mortem of this attack concluded that all 21 had exploded on impact because of a fusing issue. US Secretary of Defense Casper Weinberger and Brigadier General Thomas Tobin USAF were surprised by the use of 'dumb bombs', as on 24 May John Nott had requested 150,000 sq yd of AM-2 airfield matting for Stanley airport.[19] This had been approved and redirected from the US Marine Corps war reserve.

18   Earlier that morning of 12 June 1982, Miguel Silva had lost Diego Bellinzona of GADA 601, assigned to the TPS-44 radar, from Royal Navy shells; he was the last technician to be lost by the unit.

19   Washington National Records Center OSD Files, FRC 330–86–0042, UK 1982. Top Secret: Request for airport matting large enough to support Nimrod operations from an expanded Port Stanley airfield. British desire to husband anti-submarine warfare assets to protect resupply ships to the Falklands over the next few months.

At the United Nations building in New York, Generals Jose Miret and Miguel Mallea Gil met with Ambassadors Jeane Kirkpatrick and Jose Sorzano. Miret acknowledged that British ground troops were closing in on Port Stanley and Argentinian forces would be defeated in the Falklands by a world power.[20] In their estimation being defeated after a valiant fight, at least, had the advantage that it would hopefully unify the Argentines. Following a three-week ground campaign, British troops re-captured the islands' capital, Port Stanley, on 14 June, forcing the surrender of all Argentine troops.[21] Major General Jeremy Moore formally accepted the surrender of the Argentinian commander, Brigadier General Mario Menéndez, in Port Stanley at 2359Z on 14 June 2059hrs (local time). The conflict ended after 74 days. The Avro Vulcan had gone into battle for the first and last time; six months later No. 44 Squadron, the remaining operator of the Vulcan bomber disbanded although a few aircraft, converted to tankers, remained in service until March 1984.

Missions summary					
Mission	Target	Date	Primary Vulcan	Reserve Vulcan	Notes
Black Buck 1	Port Stanley airport	30 April–1 May	XM598 (Reeve)	XM607 (Withers)	XM607 Mission completed
Black Buck 2	Port Stanley airport	3–4 May	XM607 (Reeve)	XM598 (Montgomery)	Mission completed
Black Buck 3	Port Stanley airport	13–14 May	XM612 (Reeve)	None	Cancelled
Black Buck 4	Radar	28 May	XM597 (McDougall)	XM598 (Montgomery)	Aborted/ Recalled
Black Buck 5	Radar	30–31 May	XM597 (McDougall)	XM598 (Montgomery)	Mission completed
Black Buck 6	Radar	3 June	XM597 (McDougall)	XM598 (Montgomery)	Mission completed
Black Buck 7	Port Stanley airport	12 June	XM607 (Withers)	XM598 (Montgomery)	Mission completed

Other proposed Black Bucks					
Mission	Target	Date	Primary Vulcan	Reserve Vulcan	Notes
Black Buck 3 rescheduled	Argentine radar installations	15–16 May	XM612	XM598	AS.37 'Martel' radar
Unspecified Montgomery + crew	Not specified	18 May	XM612	None	Probe broke during refuelling bracket
Black Buck 1500hrs	Not specified	24–25 May	XM607	XM598	Cancelled by 18 Group Wg Cdr Ops

20 Generals Jose Miret mentions that Britain is in denial and that the air-carrier HMS *Invincible* has been damaged. This myth continues.

21 775 Argentinian soldiers had been killed in the last 24 hours. Those casualties led to an Argentinian cease fire after the realization it would be futile to continue the fight. (Ambassador Kirkpatrick's Meeting with General Ricardo Pena. Ref: USUN 1668 New York, June 16, 1982, 2332Z).

Planning for *Black Bucks* beyond the Falklands

Detailed planning for Vulcan raids on Argentine air bases with a recovery to Concepcíon, Chile, began at Northwood prior to clearance on 21 May. A route with four fuel transfer areas heading south-west from Ascension Island beyond the Falklands remained unchanged. The downward track tanker positions being the same as in previous *Black Buck* missions. At a point east of Bahía Granda, these missions would separate to go one of three ways: the first would turn west to attack the Base Aérea Militar (BAM) at Puerto San Julián which housed Daggers and A-4 Skyhawks. The base shared the facilities of San Julián commercial airport, and was one of the closest points to the Falklands. The second route was south-west towards BAM Río Gallegos, 1 mile west of the city, another commercial airport which had the longest runway in Argentina. A third route turned south-south-west towards Río Grande air base for its Super Étendard strike fighters and large Argentine Navy Marine Corps Battalion, roughly 6 miles out from the main city. All were on the east coast of Patagonia in the far south of Argentina. The justification for striking these sites was to reduce the effectiveness of the Argentine Air Force and naval air assets in carrying out attacks on the British Task Force, as well as reducing associated logistics.

Fuerza Aérea Argentina mainland bases
Group 4 San Julián: 16 A4C Skyhawks; 14 operational
Group 5 Río Gallegos: 30 A4B Skyhawks; 24 operational
Group 6 Río Grande and San Julián: 34 IAI M5 Daggers; 26 operational
Group 8 Comodoro Rivadavia and Río Gallegos: 16 Mirage IIIEA and Mirage IIID; 12 operational
Reserve El Plumerillo BAM, Mendoza: 10 F68F Sabers; 10 operational patrolling Andes mountains

The proposal was to fly one Vulcan, XM607, with a reserve, XM598, which would strike the target or targets, fly west over Argentinian territory, cross the Andes to the coast of Chile, then turn north up the Pacific coast to touch down at the Chilean port of Concepción, using the airport at Santiago, the Chilean capital, as an alternative. After refuelling and recovery the crew would fly east across the Andes, over Argentina at its maximum height, before turning on a heading north-east towards Ascension Island. This mission would require between 11 and 13 Victor tanker aircraft to refuel the Vulcans. However, the requirements for tankers to support Nimrod anti-submarine patrols in the South Atlantic, plus naval and RAF Harrier operations against targets on the Falkland Islands, placed limits on their availability.

The British Air Attaché in Washington approached the United States for the loan of Boeing KC-135 aerial tankers on 11 May, to be prepared on a standby basis. The aircraft could carry 100 tons of fuel, and transfer was by boom or underwing refuelling pods. The KC-135 had the enhanced capability to feed fuel to a damaged aircraft to enable a landing or a ditching at sea. The use of KC-135s would also make available a possible egress route from Chile to Easter Island some 2,218 miles away, to Tahiti in the Central Pacific for refuelling if French administrators were compliant. After this turnaround the Vulcans could fly north for 2,750 miles to Hawaii, then to McClellan Air Force Base, California, and on to Offutt in Nebraska before crossing into Canadian air space to refuel at Goose Bay in Newfoundland, before flying the 2,395 miles home to RAF Waddington, with Lossiemouth, in Moray, Scotland as a diversionary airfield. The route would avoid overflying any hostile South American countries.

The ordnance of choice was 1,000lb iron bombs, parachute-retarded or ballistic version, released at low or high level as a single stick, with the minimum of spacing, using radar for aiming and release. The release in a single stick meant that only one area on the airfield was targeted. The flightpath selected would give the greatest probability of cratering the runway and inflicting maximum collateral damage to aircraft and airfield facilities.

The alternative weapon was the 1,000lb GBU-16 Paveway II laser-guided bomb, already in use by RAF Harriers with the Task Force. Target designation was essential, either by an aircraft mounting a Pave Spike target designator or by a covert operator using a lightweight device permitting them to designate specific targets: hardened hangars, dispersal areas, fuel storage, bomb storage or airfield buildings. However, the AN/AVQ-23E Pave Spike laser designators in the RAF's arsenal (used by Buccaneer S.2B strike aircraft) were first-generation targeting lasers, unable to 'see' in the dark. The raid would have to be flown in daylight, and atmospheric conditions would need to be near perfect as cloud cover, rain or smoke could make reliable designation of targets difficult or impossible. Northwood's opinion was that, as on the first *Black Bucks*, 21 1,000lb bombs would cause maximum damage and would therefore be preferable to the Lockheed Martin guided munitions.

British intelligence discovered that GADA 601 and 602 radar coverage was wider than initially expected in Patagonia. Lack of on-site intelligence meant that Northwood did not have a clear idea of how the split was organized between commercial and military airports or how they were defended, nor any guarantees that the military aircraft would even be there if an operation took place. As the bases often shared facilities with commercial airports, Northwood had to consider not only how to avoid hitting civilian targets, but how to ensure that the raids appeared proportionate. Appearing to strike commercial airports risked damaging the justice of Britain's cause.

AFTERMATH AND ANALYSIS

There is little doubt that the *Black Buck* raids, particularly the first, had important psychological effects on the Argentine conscripts and regulars. The Argentine junta's assumption that the British would not respond with force to the occupation of the islands was shattered by the first raid. Although the British Chiefs of Staff had initially raised concerns about civilian casualties, by 23 April this was outweighed by the value of Stanley airport to the Argentinians, the risks which leaving it intact would pose to Admiral Sandy Woodward's Task Force, and the RAF's confidence that the missions proposed would carry a low risk of civilian losses.

The first *Black Buck* was also seen at least in part as a deterrent, intended to create a real fear in Argentina that its mainland was vulnerable to attack, forcing it to hold back Mirage III aircraft for air defence. It was also arguably the most militarily successful of the raids, despite the early indications that the full runway length of 4,100ft at Port Stanley remained serviceable.

While the possibility of raiding Argentina would always have been politically and strategically difficult, military plans were actively underway during the Falklands War. Even as late as 25 May 1982, four days after the British amphibious assault at San Carlos, the possibility of an attack being ordered against the mainland had not been completely rejected. Clearance was given on 20 May for the Vulcan to be fitted with a load of three Paveway 1,000lb laser-guided bombs, in case a suitable mission was proposed and approved. Senior staff at No. 1 Group were considering options for Vulcan attacks on the mainland, in particular on the southern Argentine airfields that operated ground-attack and anti-ship aircraft.

Information from US Air Force officers familiar with the Argentinian Air Force suggested that their more experienced combat pilots would be posted to Mirage squadrons and that their instrument and night flying standards were extremely good. They warned that it was likely that a Vulcan would encounter fighter activity during any attack. The effectiveness of Argentina's coordination in using radar controllers in air defence to intercept at night was

Vulcan XM597 cordoned off at Río Galeão International Airport. (Moraes Filho, Brazilian Air Force)

not known. However, the effectiveness of their radar technicians and operators of GADA 601 and 602 on the Falklands should have raised concerns.

Air Commodore John Price, Director of Operations (RAF) at the Ministry of Defence, wrote to Air Marshal Sir David Craig that such an attack should be from 'about 2,000ft after a low-level penetration.' Despite the adaptation of the Vulcan for Paveway bombs, the preference at that point was for the use of unguided weapons, as suitable 'critical' targets for attack with laser-guided bombs had not yet been identified. Craig's opinion was not recorded. However, with Argentinian air power receding, but not defeated, the risks associated with a Vulcan raid against the Argentine mainland appeared to significantly outweigh the benefits – particularly the risk of undermining the international support for the British cause. Nevertheless, the Vulcan's potential was understood and considered even if it was not exploited.

With Vulcan XM597 detained in Brazil, Chief of the Air Staff Sir Michael Beetham also looked for alternative options, utilizing the Blackburn Buccaneer S.2B in its maritime strike role. David Craig had assigned to his personal staff officer the task of preparing papers, maps and charts, specifically for targeting Argentinian naval ships, with a particular emphasis on ARA *Veinticinco de Mayo* in Argentine territorial waters off the main naval base at Puerto Belgrano. The 12 Buccaneers would run the gauntlet across Argentina using land contours, en route for the Andes to land in Chile at either Santiago or Concepción near the country's capital. This, however, did not get permission to go ahead.

Final approach: about to touch down in April 1982 on Ascension Island's Wideawake single runway, which had seen air movements catapult to 400 movements per day. (Andrew D Bird Collection)

American logistical help was vital to the success of *Black Buck*. On 27 May the US Joint Staff received an informal enquiry on the potential for purchase or lease of KC-10 aircraft by British Air Attaché Ron Dick in Washington. There was concern that the RAF crews could not operate the refuelling system without first receiving appropriate training, and US involvement in either the aircraft's support or its operations would need to be worked out. Before the fighting stopped, the United States was prepared to offer two KC-10s on a 90-day lease. Air Staff were also considering the conversion of UK-owned DC-10 aircraft to a tanker configuration to meet refuelling requirements in the South Atlantic.

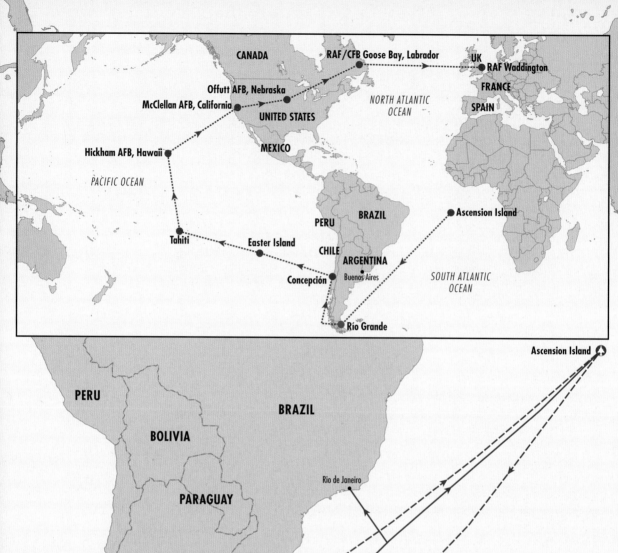

CANADA

RAF/CFB Goose Bay, Labrador

UK

RAF Waddington

FRANCE

SPAIN

Offutt AFB, Nebraska

McClellan AFB, California

UNITED STATES

NORTH ATLANTIC OCEAN

MEXICO

Hickham AFB, Hawaii

PACIFIC OCEAN

PERU

BRAZIL

Ascension Island

CHILE

ARGENTINA

Tahiti

Easter Island

Concepción

Buenos Aires

SOUTH ATLANTIC OCEAN

Río Grande

PERU

BRAZIL

BOLIVIA

PARAGUAY

Río de Janeiro

ARGENTINA

URUGUAY

CHILE

Buenos Aires

Concepción

SOUTH ATLANTIC OCEAN

Ascension Island

Trelew

San Julián

Río Gallegos

Río Grande

FALKLAND ISLANDS

South Georgia

N

0   500 miles

0   500km

Argentinian air bases

Air bases used by RAF

Total Exclusion Zone (TEZ)

Ascension–Ascension

Ascension–Chile–Ascension

Ascension–Pacific–United States–Canada–UK

OPPOSITE PROPOSED ROUTES FOR *BLACK BUCK* STRIKES ON ARGENTINA

Once the fighting was over, the defence of the Falklands would be paramount, and again US assistance was discussed. The Ministry of Defence enquired about the availability from the United States of up to 24 F-4J aircraft which would be deployed at Port Stanley. The Americans' response was that if the Ministry of Defence believed that the RAF did not have enough F-4s both to perform their NATO missions and to meet their Falklands requirements, the US would consider filling in behind British air assets in Europe before agreeing to transfer F-4Js for deployment in the Falklands.

While *Black Buck* is often thought of as the last old-fashioned RAF operation, the consideration of precision weapons for attacks against the mainland, coupled with the first combat use of laser-guided bombs by Harrier GR.3s the day before the end of the war, pointed to the future for the RAF. It demonstrated the need to ensure that capabilities were maintained through high levels of RAF training so that key skills did not evaporate, and for sufficient equipment to be available to achieve the desired effects, which required appropriate funding.

Argentina

The Argentines, of course, suffered substantial losses and had to confront serious military problems. Although they had about 240 aircraft when they invaded the Falklands, having seized the airfield, the Argentines were unable to take full advantage of it for their jet fighters. Equipment was airlifted in to extend the runway, and there was an on-site gravel pit for hardcore; however, essential bitumen was left in the hold of a merchant ship. Operating was difficult for often prosaic reasons. The state-owned airline LADE had neglected to inform the air force that Port Stanley airport had very limited facilities: there was not enough equipment to unload their Hercules efficiently, and PILLOW tanks for refuelling were blighted or obsolete.

As a result of being unable to use the airfield, Argentinian pilots raiding the Task Force faced remarkably similar situations to those encountered by Luftwaffe pilots during the Battle of Britain, where the pressure of having only five minutes in the combat zone or risking running out of fuel contributed to unforeseen accidents and human error. On 1 May, at 1315hrs (local time), Captain Gustavo Cuerva's Mirage IIIEA, which had been damaged by Lieutenant Steve Thomas, attempted to touch down at BAM Malvinas. Although he communicated his intentions clearly on VHF, the flight controller was in a state of confusion that day, nervous after suffering the Vulcan bombardment early that morning and an A 35/90 and an HS-831 of the Infanteria de Marina shot down the Mirage as it approached.

At the Comodoro Rivadavia Military Base, Argentine troops guard air defence equipment belonging to GADA 601. In the foreground is the Skyguard cabin (later hit by a Shrike missile) with Oerlikon 35mm twin cannons. (Photo by Alain Nogues/Sygma/Sygma via Getty Images)

On the Falkland Islands the Argentine defences began to falter and officers became despondent as they withdrew into Stanley. By mid-June it was obvious to Brigadier General Mario Menéndez that the Argentines could not continue the fight. A ceasefire was declared at 2215hrs (BST) on Monday 14 June, the last day of the occupation. Menéndez telephoned Galtieri and spoke of the situation and agreed to take responsibility; the surrender was finalized by 0130hrs. With the loss of the Malvinas, large demonstrations in the Argentine capital against the Galtieri junta saw the acknowledgement that elections would be the first step to a modern democracy in Argentina. Galtieri was forced to resign and Raúl Alfonsín became the first democratically elected president in 1983 after years of Argentina being under military dictatorship.

Black Buck Honours

The following airmen were awarded honours for the part they played in *Black Buck*:

- Flt Lt W F M Withers RAF, was awarded the Distinguished Flying Cross (DFC) for his part in *Black Buck 1*.
- Squadron Leader Bob Tuxford, who piloted Victor XL189 – the last Victor tanker to refuel the Vulcan prior to the raid – received the Air Force Cross.
- Tuxford's whole crew received the Queen's Commendation for Valuable Service in the Air.
- Sqdn Ldr C N McDougall RAF received the Distinguished Flying Cross (DFC) for his role in *Black Buck 6*.
- Wing Commander D. Emmerson RAF, was awarded the Air Force Cross for leadership during Operation *Corporate*, including the support of ASR during *Black Buck 1*, for the first daylight sortie off the Argentine coast in a Nimrod, and for night surveillance before Operation *Sutton*.

FURTHER READING

Blackman, Tony, *Vulcan Boys – From the Cold War to The Falklands*, Grub St., London (2007)

Blackman, Tony, *Vulcan Test Pilot – My Experiences in the Cockpit*, Grub St., London (2007)

Blackman, Tony, *Nimrod – Rise and Fall*, Grub St., London (2011)

Blackman, Tony, *Victor Boys*, Grub St., London (2012)

Brookes, Andrew, *Vulcan Units of The Cold War*, Osprey Publishing, Oxford (2009)

Chant, Christopher, *Air War in The Falklands 1982*, Osprey Publishing, Oxford (2001)

Hastings, Max & Jenkins, Simon, *The Battle for the Falklands*, Pan Macmillan, London (2022)

Middlebrook, Martin, *The Argentine Fight of the Falklands*, Pen & Sword, Barnsley (2009)

Napier, Michael, *Tornado GR1: Operational History*, Pen & Sword, Barnsley (2017)

Norman, Mike & Jones, Michael, *The Falklands War There and Back Again*, Pen & Sword, Barnsley (2019)

Phillips, Ricky D., *The First Casualty: The Untold Story of the Falklands War*, Scotland (2018)

Ramsey, Gordon, *The Falklands War: Then and Now*, Battle of Britain International, Essex (2017)

Shields, John, *Air Power in The Falklands Conflict*, Airworld, Barnsley (2021)

Southby-Tailyour, Ewen, *Exocet Falklands*, Pen & Sword, Barnsley (2014)

Tuxford, Bob, *CONTACT! A Victor Captain's Experiences in the RAF, before, during and after the Falklands Conflict*, Grub Street (2016)

White, Rowland, *Vulcan 607*, Bantam Press, London (2006)

White, Rowland, *Harrier 809*, Bantam Press, London (2020)

Woodward, Admiral Sandy, *One Hundred Days*, HarperCollins, London (1992)

INDEX